Picture Book of the
Revolution's Privateers

Picture Book of the Revolution's Privateers

By C. Keith Wilbur

Stackpole Books

PICTURE BOOK OF PRIVATEERS

Copyright © 1973 by
THE STACKPOLE COMPANY

Published by STACKPOLE BOOKS
Cameron and Kelker Streets
Harrisburg, Pa. 17105

Printed in U.S.A.

Library of Congress Cataloging in Publication Data

Wilbur, C   Keith, 1923-
   Picture book of the revolution's privateers.

      1. Privateering. 2. United States--History--
Revolution--Naval operations. I. Title.
E271.W64   973.3'5   72-10468
ISBN 0-8117-1262-1

Contents

WHERE TO FIND RELICS ILLUSTRATED
IN THIS BOOK   6

FOREWORD   7

THE COLONIALS ARM THEIR VESSELS   8

MIDGET PRIVATEERSMEN—WHALEBOATS AND
OTHER "SPIDER CATCHERS"   8

HULLS FOR SPEED AND MANEUVER   9
    "Sharp" American Hulls   The New Breed of
Privateering Ships

HOW THE HULLS WERE BUILT   10
    The Deceptively Small Colonial Shipyards
Saw Pits   Hewing and "Framing Up"   What
the Plankers and Dubbers Did   Caulking and
Scraping   Favored Ships' Colors   Stern
Finish and Fancy Carvings

FORMING AND INSTALLING THE GREAT SPARS   13

ROPES, RATLINES AND GEAR   15
    Hemp   Small Stuff   Rope   Rigging Gear

HOW THE SHIPS WERE RIGGED   16
    Standing Rigging   Deadeyes   Ratlines
Gammoning   Worming, Parcelling and
Serving   Running Rigging   Halliards
Lifts   Braces   Block and Tackle
Belaying Pins

SAILS AND SAIL RIGGINGS   20
    The Sailmaker's Tools   Seam and Rope
Stitches   Fore-and-Aft Rig   Square Rig
Sprits and Studdings for Extra Driving Power
Square Sail Seamanship—Tacking, Reefing and
Furling

PRIVATEERING—A RESPECTED
BUSINESS ENTERPRISE   25
    Who the Ship Owners Were   Privateering
Commissions   Requirements for Posting
Bond   Key Man—the Ship's Captain   The
Crew—Landlubbers, Marine Guard, Seamen
and Officers   Shares   Articles of
Agreement

THE TYPICAL CREW MEMBER   32
    His Clothing and Ditty Bag   The Bedlam of
Sounds on Shipboard   Saluting the
Quarterdeck

PUTTING OUT TO SEA   35
    Weighing Anchor   Why the Cable Crisis
Provision   Standard Watch Schedules
Time and the Ship's Bell   Advice for Topmen
Below Deck—Living Conditions and Crew
Quarters

THE SHIP'S CANNONS   44
    Gun Drills   Typical Projectiles   "Quakers"
and Wooden Armament   Carronades for
Close Work   Typical Instructions for Gunners
Miniature Cannon or Swivel Guns

LIFE ON THE HIGH SEAS   50
    The Ship's Cook, the Crew and Their Bill of
Fare   Shipboard Spare Time Hobbies
Privateering Songs   Superstitions and Ships'
Figureheads   Religion and the Seamen of
the Day

COLORS AND SIGNALS   56
    False Flag Tricks   The Signals Used for
Important Communications

IDENTIFYING THE ENEMY   58
    Convoys   Swift-Sailing Merchantmen

NAVIGATION   59
    Latitude and Determining Position by Use of
Quadrant   Longitude and Sailing Deliberately
to Side of Destination   Determining Position
by Deduction   Heaving the Log   Heaving
the Lead   Compass Courses and Allowing
for Wind and Leeway   The Captain's Charts

CHASE DECISIONS   66
    Rules for Favorable and Unfavorable Situations
Tactics for Various Wind and Other
Considerations   Bluffing—Occasionally a
Successful Tactic

BATTLE AT SEA   68
    Battle Stations and the Duties of Various Crew
Members   The Fighting Tops as Small
Fortresses   Boarding—the Privateer's
Specialty   Calculated Collisions   Grappling
Procedure   Rules for Various Boarding
Situations   Three Boarding Adventures
Instructions for Fighting Fires   Stopping
Leaks   How Various Repairs Were Made
Sea Surgery and Cook Book Medicine

THE CAPTURED PRIVATEERSMEN   80
    Their Treatment and Interrogation   Prison
Life at Forten Prison   Old Mill Prison
Educational Programs   Escape Schemes and
Rewards   Prisoner Exchanges
Independence Day Celebrations   Friends of
the Prisoners—the English Citizenry
Infamous Prison Ships—the "Whitby" and the
"Jersey"   Other Prisons—Nova Scotia,
Antigua and Jamaica   Treatment of Captured
British Seamen

PRIVATEERING ENGAGEMENTS ASHORE
AND IN HARBORS   88
    The "General Putnam" and Action Near Saco
Harbor   Captain Barlow's Exploits in
Nantucket Harbor   Commando-like Raids on
the English Coast and Nova Scotia   The "Gut"
Engagement in Boston Harbor

HOW THE SHIPS WERE SCRAPED AND REFITTED   89

PRIZE DISPOSALS AND PAY-OFFS   91
    Sale of Captured Vessels and Cargoes in
France and Spain   Court of Justice and Sales
Procedure in America   Some Sample
Staggering Profits   Fluctuating Currency and
Share Values   The Private Sea War Lost by
Great Britain

INDEX   93

Where to Find Relics Illustrated in This Book

(*Note:* The entries in this guide are arranged, in consecutive order, according to the pages on which the relics are illustrated in this book.)

7   *Privateering commission seal.* From insert reproduction (original owned by C. I. Brown) opposite page 10, *Privateers and Militia 1779-1811,* Old South Leaflets, published by the directors of Old South Work, Old South meeting-house, Boston, Mass. (n.d.)

10   *Shipyard dioramas.* In Skenesboro Museum, Whitehall, N.Y. and Peabody Museum, Salem, Mass.

10   *Pit saw.* In Peabody Museum, Salem, Mass.

11   *Felling axe, broad axe, adze.* In collections of Northampton Historical Society, Northampton, Mass.

12   *Spiral auger, spoon bits* (from gunboat *Philadelphia,* Lake Champlain, N.Y., 1776). In Smithsonian Institution, Washington, D.C.

12   *Caulking hammer and making iron.* In Portsmouth Naval Museum, Portsmouth, Va.

12   *Hawsing iron, plane and scrapers.* In Peabody Museum, Salem, Mass.

15   *Grease horn, rigger's knife and marlingspike.* In Peabody Museum, Salem, Mass.

17   *Serving mallet.* In Peabody Museum, Salem, Mass.

20   *Seamer palm, seam rubber, fid, pricker, stabber.* In Penobscot Marine Museum, Searsport, Maine.

20   *Needle holder and sailmaker's knife.* In Peabody Museum, Salem, Mass.

25   *Elias Derby* and *Capt. John Carnes.* The former from a portrait by James Frothingham and the latter from a portrait by an unknown artist, both in Peabody Museum, Salem, Mass.

27   *Capt. Hugh Hill's spyglass and quadrant in wooden box.* In collections of Beverly Historical Society, Beverly, Mass.

28   *Light seaman's cutlass.* In Philadelphia Maritime Museum.

28   *Belt pistol.* In Mariners' Museum, Newport News, Va.

28   *Ship's chest of Capt. Benjamin Cox, 1770.* In Peabody Museum, Salem, Mass.

32   *Seaman's wide-brimmed hat.* In Peabody Museum, Salem, Mass.

33   *Scissors* (from H.M.S. *Augusta,* sunk in Delaware River in 1777 in attack on Fort Mifflin). In Philadelphia Maritime Museum.

33   *Jackknife* (from H.M.S. *Augusta,* sunk in Delaware River in 1777 in attack on Fort Mifflin). In Philadelphia Maritime Museum; also at Washington's Headquarters, Newburg, N.Y.

33   *Ditty box.* In Peabody Museum, Salem, Mass.

33   *Ditty bag* (belonging to Capt. Reuben Chase, who served with John Paul Jones on the *Bon Homme Richard* in sea fight with H.M.S. *Serapis* off east coast of England, 1779). In Nantucket Whaling Museum, Nantucket, Mass.

33   *Wooden shaving dish and razor.* At Fort Ticonderoga, Ticonderoga, N.Y.

34   *Bo'sun's pipe.* In Peabody Museum, Salem, Mass.

34   *Captain's speaking trumpet.* In Peabody Museum, Salem, Mass.

37   *Cathead* (from U.S. frigate *Constitution*). At Boston Navy Yard, Charlestown, Mass.

38   *Hanging half hour glass.* In collections of Beverly Historical Society, Beverly, Mass.

40   *Wooden cabin lantern* (used on vessels by Capt. Samuel Page of Danvers before 1750). In Peabody Museum, Salem, Mass.

40   *Wrought iron candle holder.* In Wilson Museum, Castine, Maine.

41   *Captain's bunk.* In H.M.S. *Bounty* replica, St. Petersburg, Fla.

41   *Pewter thunder jug.* In Mariners' Museum, Newport News, Va.

42   *Meat cask* (bottom of page). In Philadelphia Maritime Museum.

42   *Pewter tap* (from British warship sunk during siege of Yorktown). In Mariners' Museum, Newport News, Va.

43   *Crew's quarters.* In H.M.S. *Bounty* replica, St. Petersburg, Fla.

44   *Cannon* (from Connecticut privateer *Nancy*). In collections of New Haven Historical Society, New Haven, Conn.

45   *Wooden shot gauge* (from *Philadelphia,* 1776). In Smithsonian Institution, Washington, D.C.

45   *Wooden shoe or "sabot"* (from *Royal Savage,* Lake Champlain, 1776). In Smithsonian Institution, Washington, D.C.

45   *Iron shot gauge* (from *Philadelphia,* 1776). In Smithsonian Institution, Washington, D.C.

46   *Bar shot and chain shot.* In Saratoga Battlefield National Park, Saratoga, N.Y.

46   *Grape shot* (stored in Salem Town Hall during Revolution). In collections of Essex Institute, Salem, Mass.

46   *Canister.* In collections of Essex Institute, Salem, Mass.

46   *Langrage.* In collections of Essex Institute, Salem, Mass.

47   *Powder keg.* At Colonial Williamsburg, Williamsburg, Va.

47   *Tampion* (for *Philadelphia's* 9-pounders, 1776). In Smithsonian Institution, Washington, D.C.

48   *Copper powder measure, gunner's copper knife and powder horn.* At Fort Ticonderoga, Ticonderoga, N.Y.

48   *Powder ladle.* In Peabody Museum, Salem, Mass.

49   *Worming iron.* In Peabody Museum, Salem, Mass.

50   *Swivel gun.* In Skenesboro Museum, Whitehall, N.Y.

51   *Dried potato slices and hard tack, 1785.* In Peabody Museum, Salem, Mass.

51   *Knife and fork* (from British frigate H.M.S. *Augusta,* sunk in Delaware in 1777). In Philadelphia Maritime Museum.

51   *Pewter mug.* In collections of Northampton Historical Society, Northampton, Mass.

52   *Sailor's pipe.* In Peabody Museum, Salem, Mass.

52   *Iron clam rake.* In the author's collection.

52   *Fish or eel spear.* At Fort Ticonderoga, Ticonderoga, N.Y.

53   *Broadside, "Manly. A Favorite New Song in the American Fleet."* In Peabody Museum, Salem, Mass.

54   *Image of devil.* From painting *An Effigy of Arnold paraded in Philadelphia* by Charles Willson Peale in Metropolitan Museum of Art.

54   *Sea serpents* (from map by Olaus Magnus, 1539). Reproduced on page 23 of *The American Heritage History of the Thirteen Colonies.*

54   *Derwent lion.* In the Mariners' Museum, Newport News, Va.

55   *Privateer figurehead* (from brigantine *Jolly Tar,* 1781). In the Mariners' Museum, Newport News, Va.

59   *Hadley's reflecting quadrant.* In Portsmouth Naval Museum, Portsmouth, Va.

60   *Pocket compass and sun dial.* In the author's collection.

61   *Log board, half minute glass and log line.* In the Peabody Museum, Salem, Mass.

62   *Fathom leads.* In Peabody Museum, Salem, Mass.

63   *Exploded view of ship's compass.* In Peabody Museum, Salem, Mass.

64   *Dog vane.* In Peabody Museum, Salem, Mass.

65   *Dividers and protractor.* In Peabody Museum, Salem, Mass.

66   *Telescopes.* In Peabody Museum, Salem, Mass.

67   *Wooden thole pin* (from British warship sunk during siege of Yorktown). In Mariners' Museum, Newport News, Va.

68   *Capt. Haraden.* From miniature painting in Peabody Museum, Salem, Mass.

68   *Battle rattle.* At Fort Ticonderoga, Ticonderoga, N.Y.

68   *Officer's pewter whistle.* In collection of Paul Patterson, M.D., Albany, N.Y.

69   *Boarding pike.* In Peabody Museum, Salem, Mass.

69   *Privateer sword.* In Custom House, Salem, Mass.

69   *Iron pike head.* In West Point Museum, West Point, N.Y.

70   *Cast iron hand grenade.* In Smithsonian Institution, Washington, D.C.

70   *Cohorn.* In collections of Essex Institute, Salem, Mass.

70   *Ship's arms chest.* In H.M.S. *Bounty* replica, St. Petersburg, Fla.

70   *American rifle, British sea-service musket.* In Colonial Williamsburg, Williamsburg, Va. and Smithsonian Institution, Washington, D.C., respectively.

75   *Privateer blunderbuss.* At U.S. Naval Academy, Annapolis, Md.

75   *British naval boarding pistol.* In Smithsonian Institution, Washington, D.C.

75   *British boarding axe.* In Philadelphia Maritime Museum.

75   *Boat hook.* At Fort Ticonderoga, Ticonderoga, N.Y.

77   *Pitch brush and pitch dish* (from *Philadelphia,* 1776). In Smithsonian Institution, Washington, D.C.

78   *Screw tourniquet.* At Morristown National Historical Park, Morristown, N.J.

78   *Retractor.* In collection of Armed Forces Institute of Pathology, Washington, D.C.

78   *Tenaculum* (belonging to Dr. Solomon Drowne). At Fort Ticonderoga, Ticonderoga, N.Y.

78   *Crooked needle.* At Fort Ticonderoga, Ticonderoga, N.Y.

78   *Amputation saw.* In the author's collection.

78   *Scalpel* (belonging to Dr. Solomon Drowne). At Fort Ticonderoga, Ticonderoga, N.Y.

79   *Medicine chest* (belonging to Dr. Joshua Fisher). In collections of Beverly Historical Society, Beverly, Mass.

79   *Medicine bottles.* At Fort Ticonderoga, Ticonderoga, N.Y.

80   *Leg iron.* In Peabody Museum, Salem, Mass.

81   *Handcuffs.* At Fort Ticonderoga, Ticonderoga, N.Y.

82   *Leg irons.* At Fort Ticonderoga, Ticonderoga, N.Y.

83   *"Cat."* In Peabody Museum, Salem, Mass.

85   *British prison ship* Jersey. Suggested by picture from "Recollections of the Jersey Prison Ship," manuscript by Thomas Dring in collections of New-York Historical Society, New York, N.Y.

86   *Section of prison ship mooring chain.* In collections of New-York Historical Society.

87   *Snuff box* (made by an American prisoner aboard prison ship *Jersey*). In Philadelphia Maritime Museum.

89   *Captain James Mugford and coffin.* From the broadside "Funeral Elegy, James Mugford" in Peabody Museum, Salem, Mass.

92   *Officer.* From 1775 Massachusetts treasury note.

PORTION OF AN EMBOSSED
SEAL FROM A CONGRESSIONAL
PRIVATEERING COMMISSION.

FOREWORD

There is a gap in America's Revolutionary War history about as big as the Atlantic Ocean. On this watery highway, the mightiest naval power in the world carried soldiers and supplies enough to crush her rebellious American subjects. At the outset of the conflict, there was not a single Continental vessel to annoy the English shipping. By 1777, there were but thirty-four cruisers afloat, and in 1782 their number had been whittled to seven. Yet no enemy vessel was safe on the high seas!

A sort of civilian navy had evened the odds - the privateersmen. Outfitted at the ship owner's expense and commissioned by the new states and Congress to attack and take enemy vessels, they make a mighty contribution to America's independence. Over two thousand privately armed vessels, large and small, carried eighteen thousand cannon and seventy thousand men into battle. Their efforts brought back a grand total of sixteen warships and two thousand, nine hundred and eighty British merchant vessels. Value wise, these prizes paid off fifty million dollars to the ship owners and the volunteers making the captures. Washington's hard-pressed army received much of the war booty, while King George gained nothing but grief.

And there lies the gap in our early history, for relatively little is known of these Yankees who combined patriotism with profit. Such private and highly individualistic cruises rarely found their way into official records. Many old ship's logs, filled with the excitement of the chase, still remain undiscovered in the attics of descendants. Gleanings come from the occasional diaries and journals (and some are most remarkable in their observations), letters from shipboard or prison, contemporary newspapers reporting privateer actions or prize sales, British scale drawings of captured sharp-sailing craft, and eighteenth century texts used in gunnery, navigation and surgery.

When these fragments were gathered, sorted, and spliced into the following pages, the privateersman of two hundred years ago stands tall among his liberty-loving countrymen. He is well worth knowing better!

IF IT FLOATS ~ ARM IT!

Through the years, American shipyards had developed fast and highly maneuverable small vessels to compete with the more sluggish European cargo ship. With a few changes, these craft made decent enough privateersmen. First, bulwarks must be pierced (hopefully, the cannon would be located). The magazine must be outsized, placed in the hull and made of the most up-to-date anti-fire construction. This was one of the most expensive changes. Shot lockers were built. Decks must be reinforced to withstand the cannon's recoil. The crews quarters must be enlarged for a greater number of crewmen. The shipyards were not found wanting. It was a rare vessel that could not be converted into a privately armed ship in several weeks.

THE "SPIDER CATCHERS" ~

One needn't have the wealth and resources of the ship owners to take part in this great ocean-going bonanza. A number of enterprising citizens might pool a small amount of capital and man their own small armed boat. Whaleboats were preferred, although barges and other small open craft were also used. Few "Spider Catchers", as they were called, were more than thirty feet in length, and most were of eight to ten tons burthen. Many were decked for longer excursions. They carried eight or more oars and often held a sail as well. Usually a swivel gun - and sometimes a small cannon - was mounted in the bow. The crew ranged from less than a dozen to thirty or more. Most were armed with pistols and muskets - or at least a sword.

These small boats grew in numbers as the war for Independence progressed. They worked well together - a bit unusual for the average privateersman - and a flotilla of four or five presented a combined firepower that could hit an enemy vessel from many sides at once. Merchantmen, transports, supply ships and occasionally an armed vessel of fair size fell into their bag of prizes.

Nantucket and Vineyard Sounds off New England, Long Island Sound, and the Chesapeake Bay areas were favorite haunts for the whaleboat privateersmen. But busiest of all was the entire New Jersey coastline and New York Bay. Perhaps this was largely due to Adam Hyler of New Jersey, one of our most famous flotillamen. As soon as the British had occupied New York City in 1776, Hyler led his swarm of hornets between Egg Harbor and Staten Island. Occasionally one of his boats fell victim to those sent out by the British fleet, but new ones were quickly built as replacements. Hyler's activities were the greatest between the years of 1781 and 1782.

"SHARP" AMERICAN HULLS

The average cargo vessel of the eighteenth century was bulky by nature. Resembling a wooden box set adrift, they were the beasts of burden on the high seas. But there were those American merchant craft that were decidedly _not_ average. They were small and sleek, and rather frankly designed to do service in smuggling or illegal trading. The Crown's restrictive trade acts had long been out-maneuvered and out-sailed by these sharp-hulled sailors. Those from New England carried a higher freeboard to take on the sloppy North Atlantic weather while those built in the Chesapeake Bay region needed less height above the calmer southern seas. But aside from a few regional differences, they carried similar stream-lined profiles. Converted to privateersmen, they initially took a heavy toll of British wartime shipping.

THE SPEEDY SHARP-BUILT HULL. THE TOPSAIL SCHOONER RIG WAS A FAVORITE.

THE NEW PRIVATEER BREED ~ The enemy reacted quickly by placing more armament aboard his cargo ships and

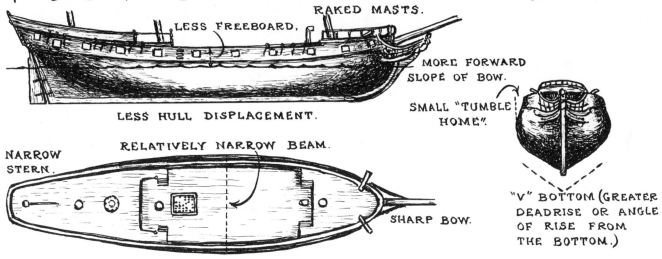

RAKED MASTS.

LESS FREEBOARD.

MORE FORWARD SLOPE OF BOW.

LESS HULL DISPLACEMENT.

RELATIVELY NARROW BEAM.

SMALL "TUMBLE HOME".

NARROW STERN.

SHARP BOW.

"V" BOTTOM (GREATER DEADRISE OR ANGLE OF RISE FROM THE BOTTOM.)

sending over more of the Royal Navy on convoy and watch-dog duty. By early in 1776, the shipyards along the American coastline were busy with the answer. The sharp lines of the New England and Chesapeake swift vessels were enlarged into a privateer built specifically for the purpose. Actually, no hull was built to exceed one hundred and twenty feet in length. They were still small enough to carry whatever rig struck one's fancy, be it schooner, brig, brigantine, snow or whatever. And under that spread of sail was the sharp hull that would pleasure any privateering captain.

Storage space was decreased, for there were fewer provisions and less ammunition needed for short cruises. Prize goods taken aboard would include only the valuable smaller items. Cannon that lined the deck were small bore and lighter requiring less "tumble home" to bring weight toward the center of the hull. Less recoil required less reinforcing timber. Cannon and like poundage were kept free of the bow and stern to eliminate added displacement and heavier, rounded ends. With weight lessened, the hull could be of relatively light construction and cost.

There were, however, two weighty considerations that were willingly added. Spars and rigging must be plentiful enough to fill the sky with canvas. An outsized crew must be ready to handle the sails and rigging, man the cannons, supply sharp-shooting marines, and still have enough hands for boarding, prize crews and guards aplenty for prisoners. Any privateersman would tell you that these were necessities, not luxuries.

SHIPYARDS

The colonial shipyard was deceptively small. There was just about room enough for two or three vessels on the ways, stacks of lumber in various stages of seasoning (although the privateering boom gave little chance for aging), and a rope and sail loft. That was all. But crammed into this plot of real estate were sawyers, carpenters, dubbers, planking gangs, painters, rope and sail specialists and finish carpenters - all bringing their specialized skills to the new vessel.

Proposed naval ships for the young nation often went a-begging. Investors in a privateer could dig deeply and pay a much more handsome wage to these ships' craftsmen. With Continental paper the victim of galloping inflation, the ship was frequently purchased in bulk merchandise. Butter, rum, salt and tobacco were good as gold. And they received solid value, for these were the light and fast vessels that might soon bring the war to the King's own shores.

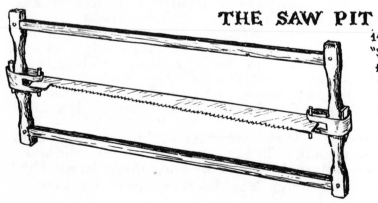

THE SAW PIT ~ Raw logs were turned into lengths of planking by "saw gangs" of three or four men. Planks for the skin and decks were frequently sixty feet long and several inches in thickness. The pit saw that bit its way through these distances of wood carried a blade four or five feet in length. This was held in a rectangular

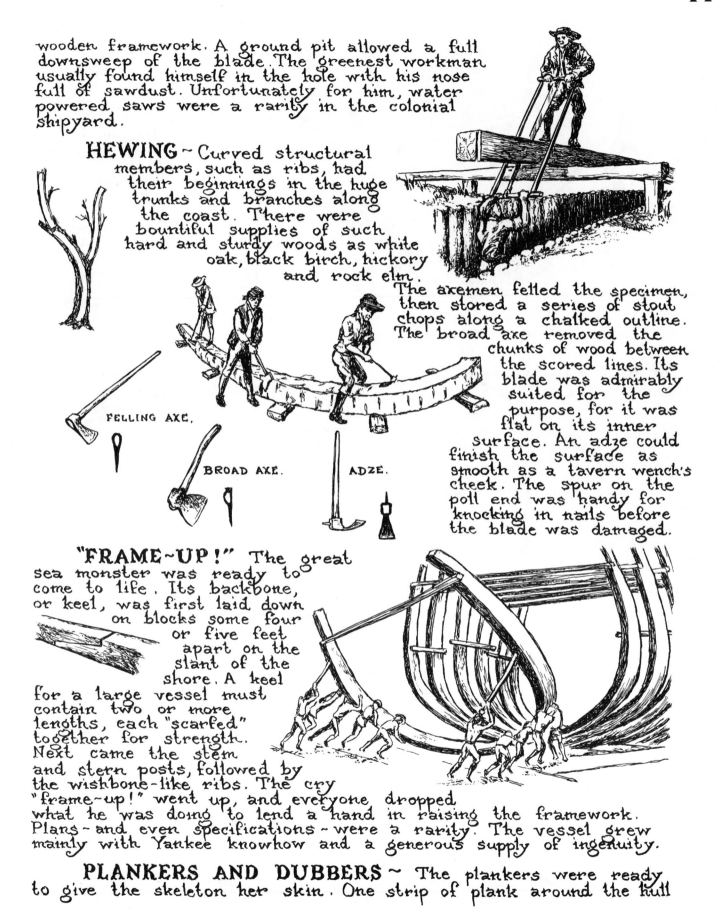

wooden framework. A ground pit allowed a full downsweep of the blade. The greenest workman usually found himself in the hole with his nose full of sawdust. Unfortunately for him, water powered saws were a rarity in the colonial shipyard.

HEWING ~
Curved structural members, such as ribs, had their beginnings in the huge trunks and branches along the coast. There were bountiful supplies of such hard and sturdy woods as white oak, black birch, hickory and rock elm.

FELLING AXE.

BROAD AXE.   ADZE.

The axemen felled the specimen, then stored a series of stout chops along a chalked outline. The broad axe removed the chunks of wood between the scored lines. Its blade was admirably suited for the purpose, for it was flat on its inner surface. An adze could finish the surface as smooth as a tavern wench's cheek. The spur on the poll end was handy for knocking in nails before the blade was damaged.

"FRAME~UP!"
The great sea monster was ready to come to life. Its backbone, or keel, was first laid down on blocks some four or five feet apart on the slant of the shore. A keel for a large vessel must contain two or more lengths, each "scarfed" together for strength. Next came the stem and stern posts, followed by the wishbone-like ribs. The cry "frame-up!" went up, and everyone dropped what he was doing to lend a hand in raising the framework. Plans ~ and even specifications ~ were a rarity. The vessel grew mainly with Yankee knowhow and a generous supply of ingenuity.

PLANKERS AND DUBBERS ~
The plankers were ready to give the skeleton her skin. One strip of plank around the hull

was known as a streak. A good planking gang could make two streaks of plank in a day. But before a plank could fit snugly against the frame, each rib edge must be gently curved. This was the job of the dubber. His adze must be sharp enough to shave the sunburn off a sailor's chin. The streaks were secured to the ribs with hickory or locust tree-nails (trunnels). Holes for the purpose were bored at about one and one eighth inches in diameter with long augers. Spikes and other iron wear were much too scarce to be used to any extent on privately owned ships.

SPIRAL AUGER

SPOON BITS OR DOWEL-BITS FROM THE CONTINENTAL GUNBOAT "PHILADELPHIA"- LAKE CHAMPLAIN, 1776.

CAULKING AND SCRAPING ~ Oakum (tarred hemp) and
cotton were driven in between the streaks to make the hull waterproof. The sharp ringing sound of the mallet against the hawzing irons was enough to shake a seagull's tail feathers loose.

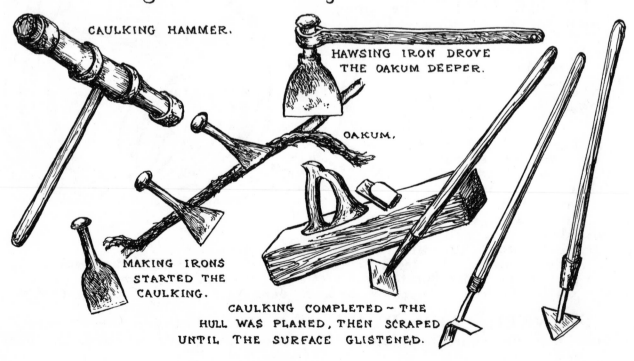

CAULKING HAMMER.

HAWSING IRON DROVE THE OAKUM DEEPER.

OAKUM.

MAKING IRONS STARTED THE CAULKING.

CAULKING COMPLETED ~ THE HULL WAS PLANED, THEN SCRAPED UNTIL THE SURFACE GLISTENED.

FAVORED COLORS ~ Paint placed a barrier between the newly crafted hull and the destructive sea water. And it did more, for the colors dressed the privateer in a blaze of finery. Earth pigments were abundant in the colonies. Iron oxide had colored landlocked barns their characteristic "barn red" for generations. It was no less a favorite with seafarers. Sienna and yellow ochre also held their own on the ocean. Lamp black was easy to come by, but many of the blues and greens were imported. White paint rarely entered the privateer's color scheme, for it was expensive and dried with an off-yellow tint.

The color scheme was as individualistic as the vessel that wore it. But more usual combinations were yellow or brown hulls with a black stripe, or black hulls with a yellow or white line between the wales. Gun ports were definitely not painted black.

The checkered painting originated some years later under Lord Nelson's command. American Revolutionary privateersmen would look dimly on his vessel looking like anything other than an innocent merchantman.

WALES

NANCY

BALTIMORE

Only when he was hard by his quarry would be run out the black snouts of his cannon for action.

Below the water line, tallow was frequently in service. A formula of the times called for "paying" the bottom with one part tallow, one part brimstone, and three parts resin. Copper sheathing was, of course, the last word in underwater surfacing. First used in 1760, it discouraged the hungriest of sea worms. But a privateer had as much chance of sheathing his hull with this scarce metal as he would receiving a commendation from King George III.

STERN FINISH ~ Fancy carvings were a rarity on the privately owned war vessel. A few scrolls and flourishes did find their way to the stern counter. There, the privateer proudly displayed her name. Immediately below was her port of registry.

SPARS

Spars were those great poles that supported the ship's canvas ~ masts, bowsprit, yards, booms and the like. The resinous pines and spruces grew tall and straight in North America ~ a bonus

that was not unappreciated by Mother England's ship-wrights. Those giants that measured twentyfour or more inches in diameter ~ a foot above the ground ~ were marked for royal use by the King's broad arrow. Pre-revolutionary colonists had never been overly conscientious in honoring their sovereign's ownership mark. Such trees were cut into planks of less than the tell-tale twentyfour inch width.

Ship's timber was best air seasoned. Not so with the spars, however. The great "sticks" were pickled in the brine of nearby tidal creeks. There the resinous woods were kept sound and resilient. At this outsized play-yard, local youngsters skipped about on the floating mammoths like so many chipmunks. And when a "stick" had been selected and

dry-docked on wooden supports. The children could scratch one end of the trunk and transmit the sound perfectly to waiting ears at the other end. The conflict of their elders seemed far away.

The hundred or so feet of future mast must be debarked and then hewed square. Knots and other irregularities were thereby removed. The edges of this great four-sided log were next beveled into an octagonal cross section. Each face must be equidistant from the center of the pole ~ an uncommon skill by any yardstick.

The new mast was then rounded and smoothed with draw knives and planes. A rule of thumb called for a mast to be hewed to a length of as many yards as there were inches at the butt. Therefore, thirty-six inches across the base would mean a total length of thirtysix yards. For stepping a mainmast to a specific hull, the over-all mast should be three times the footage of the beam.

The masts were stepped after launching, and were hoisted in place from the yard dock.

"LEARNING THE ROPES"

The sailor was a jack-tar of all trades. At sea, he was expected to be both a rigger and sailmaker. Vicious winds or enemy action might be just over the horizon, ready to test his skills. On board, "knowing the ropes" was a life or death matter with the privateersman. T'was no idle phrase.

HEMP had no equal. The fibers between the bark and pith of the Cannabis sativa plant could carry the greatest weights, yet lost none of its strength when tarred. Sea water could not make it swell, and the hemp handled well in any condition.

"SMALL STUFF" was any cordage less than an inch in circumference. The number of threads (yarns) that made it up determined its name ~ as nine-thread stuff.

ROPE was an inch or more in circumference, and there were three standard twists or lays.

STRAND

YARNS

HAWSER~LAID ROPE~
THREE STRANDS
TWISTED RIGHT-HANDED

(LEFT TO RIGHT).

SHROUD~LAID
FOUR STRANDS
TWISTED RIGHT-HANDED
ABOUT A CENTER CORE
GAVE GREAT STRENGTH
TO STANDING RIGGING.

CABLE ~ LAID =
THREE HAWSER
LAID ROPES LAID UP
TOGETHER LEFT-HANDED.
USED WHERE ELASTICITY
NEEDED.

RIGGING GEAR ~ Three basic tools needed.

3. RIGGER'S KNIFE~
WAS THICK~BLADED AND
SQUARE~ENDED.

CORDAGE WAS CUT
ON A SPAR BY A SHARP
BLOW OF THE MARLING~
SPIKE HEAD ON THE
KNIFE. A GOOD RIGGER
COULD CUT ALL BUT TWO
STRANDS WITHOUT SCORING
THE SPAR.

1. GREASE HORN ~
HELD TALLOW
FOR GREASING STRANDS.

2. MARLINGSPIKE ~ A LONG IRON SPIKE
THAT OPENED STRANDS FOR SPLICING AND
KNOT TYING. A LANYARD HOLE WAS BELOW THE HEAD.

SHIP'S RIGGING

Shipboard rope looked like tangled seaweed to the landsman. Yet not a strand was without reason. Even the twist or lay determined how an eye splice was made, a dead-eye turned in, or how a rope was seized to itself. And no proper seaman would call his cordage "rope". Each was named according to its function — stays, shrouds, halyards, lifts and braces, for example.

The rigging must support or pull considerable topside weight. Hemp was a happy choice, for a single yarn could support a hundred pounds. Two kinds of rigging did the job. Even the greenest volunteer could spot the difference from dockside. The standing rigging was as black as its tar-coating could make it. The lines were taut and well-secured. The running rigging, on the other hand, was its own natural yellow color and gently curved on the movable blocks.

STANDING RIGGING

Here was the permanent cordage that supported the masts and bowsprit, secured firmly with deadeyes.

STAYS SECURE MASTS FORE AND AFT.

SHROUDS SECURE MASTS FROM SIDE TO SIDE.

DEADEYES

DEADEYES WERE CUT FROM HARD WOOD, FREQUENTLY ELM.

THE STANDING RIGGING WAS TIGHTENED BY ROVING A LAN-YARD THROUGH THE EYES.

THE LANYARD WAS SNUGGED UP WITH A BLOCK AND TACKLE, THEN TIED TO THE STANDING RIGGING.

RATLINES ~ the shrouds served
as a ladder for going aloft a well as
supporting the masts. The fifteen or
sixteen inch spacing made a convenient
step interval.

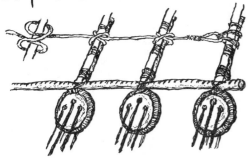

THE CHANNEL WAS A HEAVY PLANK
THAT PROJECTED FROM THE HULL. IT
GAVE GREATER SPREAD TO THE SHROUDS
TO CARRY THEM CLEAR OF THE BULWARKS.

GAMMONING ~ was
a different sort of standing
rigging, designed to
hold down the
bowsprit.

WORMING, PARCELLING, AND SERVING
The standing rigging was
protected from weather
and wear.

WORMING ~
SPUNYARN OR
SMALL CORD IS WORMED
INTO THE HOLLOWS BE-
TWEEN STRANDS TO KEEP
OUT MOISTURE AND TO
SMOOTH THE ROPE FOR
PARCELLING.

PARCELLING ~ STRIPS OF
OLD TARRED CANVAS
BOUND THE ROPE AND
FURTHER WATERPROOFED
THE STANDING RIGGING.

SERVING ~ SPUNYARN
BOUND THE ROPE WITH
A SERVING MALLET FOR
THE FINAL PROTECTING
SURFACE.

MARLINGSPIKES SERVED
AND REPAIRED EYE
SPLICES.

A SERVING BOARD ALSO
WAS USED FOR THE EYES.

"WORM AND PARCEL
WITH THE LAY
BUT ALWAYS SERVE
THE OTHER WAY."

RUNNING RIGGING

The running rigging was made up of those movable ropes that changed the position of the sails and their supporting spars (yards) on square riggers. All running rigging ran through moving blocks, and therefore could not have the protective tar coating of the standing rigging.

Running rigging could pivot, raise or lower the spars. There were three basic kinds.

1. HALLIARDS (or "haul-yards") raised or lowered yards.

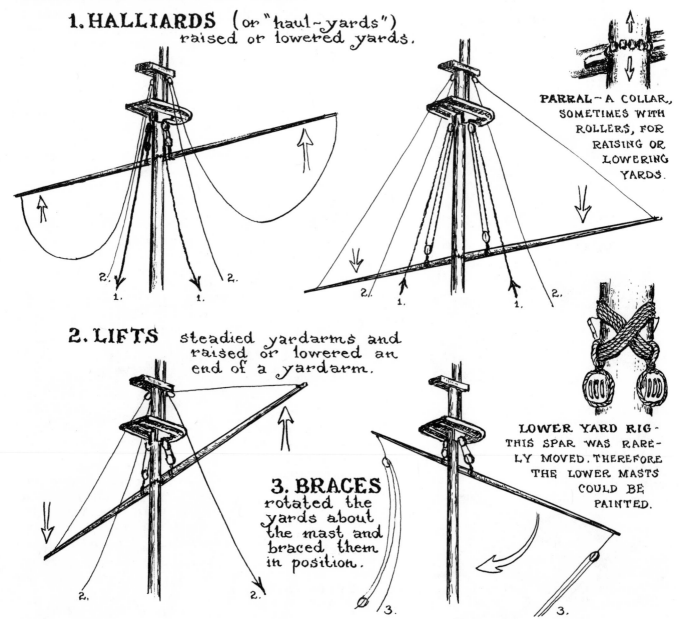

PARRAL – A COLLAR, SOMETIMES WITH ROLLERS, FOR RAISING OR LOWERING YARDS.

2. LIFTS steadied yardarms and raised or lowered an end of a yardarm.

3. BRACES rotated the yards about the mast and braced them in position.

LOWER YARD RIG- THIS SPAR WAS RARE- LY MOVED. THEREFORE THE LOWER MASTS COULD BE PAINTED.

BLOCK AND TACKLE ~ The greenest landsman

volunteer soon became fast friends with these wondrous muscle-savers! The all-wood block held a grooved wheel (shiv) through which the rope (tackle) was rove. A privateer would carry nothing larger than a three shiv block.

SHELL.   SHIV.   PIN.   BLOCK STRAPPING.   SINGLE SHIV BLOCK.   DOUBLE SHIV BLOCK.

FIDDLE BLOCK LIES FLATTER TO YARD OR MAST THAN DOUBLE-SHIV BLOCK.

The block and tackle made the running rigging more efficient in several ways. A rope's direction could be changed to a position of easier hauling. A single fixed block had no power advantage, however.

More important, blocks could be used in combination to lift or move great weights with less effort. One block was fixed to the ship itself, and the movable block attached to the spar or other object to be moved. The number of ropes entering or leaving the MOVABLE block determined the amount of power gained. If the "fall" is attached to the moving block, an additional advantage is gained.

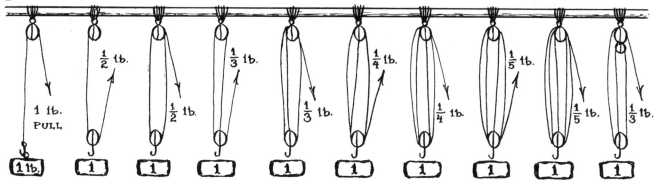

BELAYING PIN ~

After passing through the blocks, the running rigging was brought to the deck. There, the free ends were fastened temporarily to the belaying pins in the pinrails. It was made fast, or "belayed" by twisting one or two figure of eights about the pin. The running rigging could be released in a moment's notice.

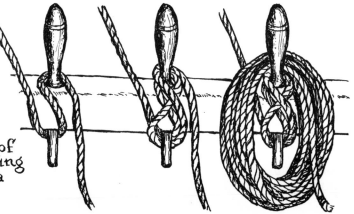

SAILS ~ OR "SHIP'S CLOTHING"

During the Revolution, sail cloth was imported from Europe-and occasionally from the East. In the colonies, there were no mills for its manufacture until the first at Beverly, Massachusetts in 1788. "Oznabrig" was favored-a coarse linen originating in Oznaburg, Germany! Every shipyard had its sailmaker's loft. On its expanse of floor, the sail cloth was chalked out in its various shapes and sizes. Then the sailmaker's palms and needles would busy over the massive yardage. There was much to be done, for no right-thinking privateer captain would put to sea without an extra "suit" of sails.

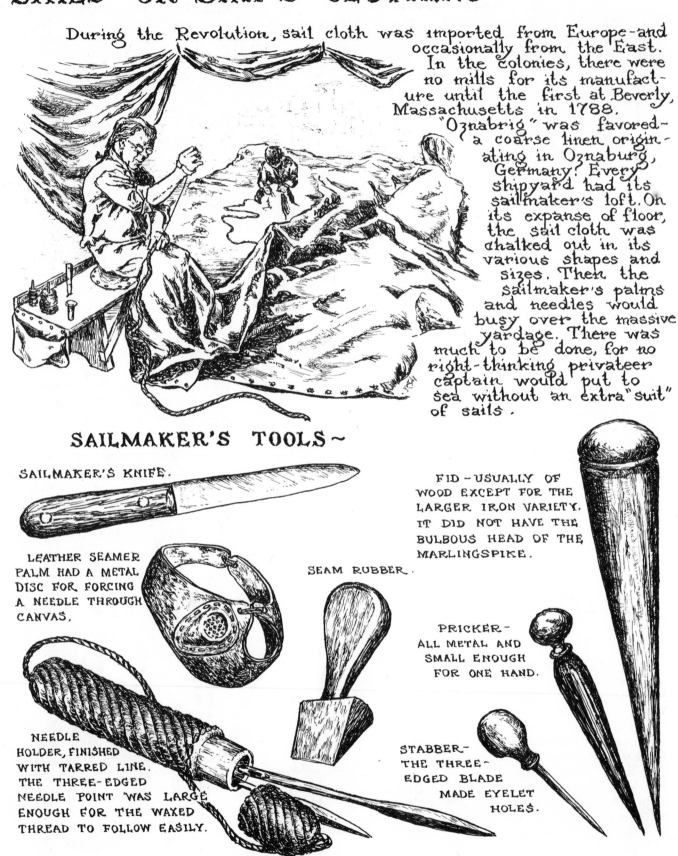

SAILMAKER'S TOOLS ~

SAILMAKER'S KNIFE.

LEATHER SEAMER PALM HAD A METAL DISC FOR FORCING A NEEDLE THROUGH CANVAS.

SEAM RUBBER.

FID ~ USUALLY OF WOOD EXCEPT FOR THE LARGER IRON VARIETY. IT DID NOT HAVE THE BULBOUS HEAD OF THE MARLINGSPIKE.

PRICKER - ALL METAL AND SMALL ENOUGH FOR ONE HAND.

NEEDLE HOLDER, FINISHED WITH TARRED LINE. THE THREE-EDGED NEEDLE POINT WAS LARGE ENOUGH FOR THE WAXED THREAD TO FOLLOW EASILY.

STABBER - THE THREE-EDGED BLADE MADE EYELET HOLES.

SEAM AND ROPING STITCHES~

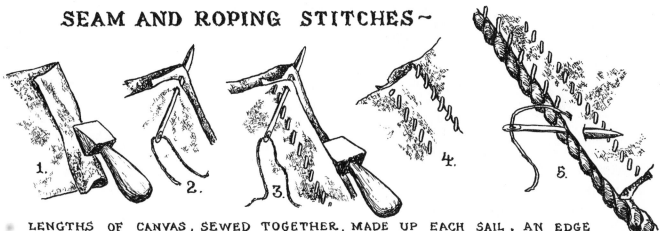

LENGTHS OF CANVAS, SEWED TOGETHER, MADE UP EACH SAIL. AN EDGE IS FIRST TURNED AND CREASED WITH THE "SEAM RUBBER" (1). THE ADJOINING CLOTH IS SEWED TO THE CREASE (2). THE JOINED LENGTHS WERE TURNED OVER AND THE STITCH WAS REPEATED (3.). RESULTING DOUBLE ROW OF STITCHES (4) WAS KNOWN AS A "FLAT SEAM". A ROPE - THE BOLTROPE (5) WAS SEWED AROUND THE EDGES OF THE FINISHED SAIL TO STRENGTHEN IT.

SAIL RIGS

The canvas dress that made the vessel a real lady also supplied her driving power. The privateer crowded as much into the sky as was possible, for speed was the first consideration. And there were two different rigs to think upon, each with its own advantages. The swift and seawise captain would likely find both the fore-and-aft and the square rig to his liking.

FORE-AND-AFT RIG ~ These were the sails that ran down the center of the vessel and were hoisted on gaff and boom or on the standing stay lines. The schooner and sloop were favored by the privateersmen with their fore-and-aft rigs. Often square sails were added for more versatility. A square rigged vessel would, for the same reason, carry a gaff and boom spanker aft and sails between the masts and bowsprit.

-SCHOONER -
A FAST, MANEUVERABLE ALL-AMERICAN RIG. CARRIED TWO OR THREE MASTS WITH FORE-AND-AFT SAILS.

-SLOOP-
A SMALLER, SINGLE MASTED SISTER TO THE SWIFT SCHOONER.

FORE-AND-AFT STAYSAILS ON SQUARE RIGGER. THE SPANKER ON GAFF AND BOOM IS AFT.

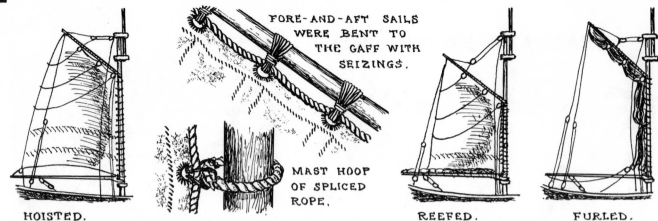

FORE-AND-AFT SAILS WERE BENT TO THE GAFF WITH SEIZINGS.

MAST HOOP OF SPLICED ROPE.

HOISTED.

REEFED.

FURLED.

The fore-and-aft stern sail was counterbalanced by the bowsprit sails. The stays that supported the bowsprit also helped. These were called the jibs. Old sea hands could tell the who and where of a distant vessel by the "cut of her jib."

Advantages to this rig were many. It was decidedly more weatherly than the square rig, for it could sail close to the wind - nearly into it - with little side drift or leeway. Faster time could therefore be made on a windward course. Narrow channels or confined areas were handily covered by range of maneuverability. The fore-and-aft could come about easily without losing way. And lastly, relatively few crewmen were needed to handle the sail. All in all, it was a happy addition to any privateering vessel.

SQUARE RIG ~ These rectangular sails were bent to the yards that extended across the width of the vessel. Hull size and spread of sail increased with privateering fever. The two favored square-riggers, the brig and the brigantine, still carried their share of fore-and-aft sails.

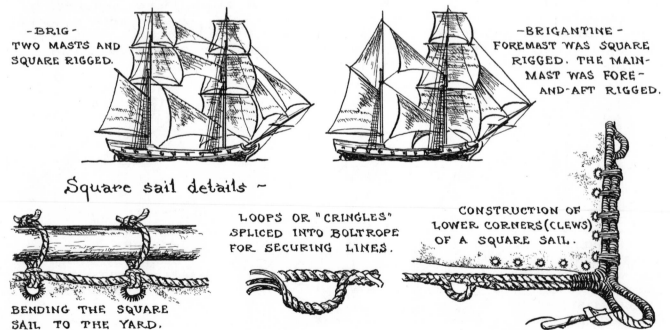

-BRIG-
TWO MASTS AND
SQUARE RIGGED.

-BRIGANTINE -
FOREMAST WAS SQUARE
RIGGED. THE MAIN-
MAST WAS FORE-
AND-AFT RIGGED.

Square sail details ~

CONSTRUCTION OF
LOWER CORNERS (CLEWS)
OF A SQUARE SAIL.

BENDING THE SQUARE
SAIL TO THE YARD.

LOOPS OR "CRINGLES"
SPLICED INTO BOLTROPE
FOR SECURING LINES.

EXTRA DRIVING POWER~
Added canvas could bring a plump prize home or a speedy retreat from a stronger enemy. The fore-and-aft sails contributed the staysails. Special square sails also gave push with the bowsprit rigging and the studding sails.

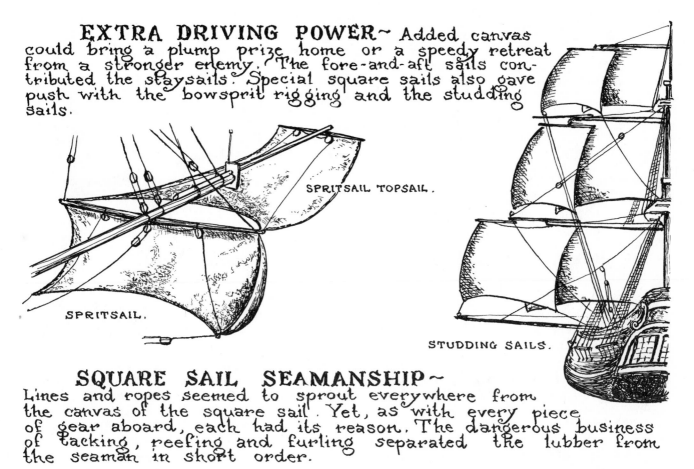

SPRITSAIL TOPSAIL.

SPRITSAIL.

STUDDING SAILS.

SQUARE SAIL SEAMANSHIP~
Lines and ropes seemed to sprout everywhere from the canvas of the square sail. Yet, as with every piece of gear aboard, each had its reason. The dangerous business of tacking, reefing and furling separated the lubber from the seaman in short order.

TACKING ~
When the ship came about on a different course, the square sails were pivoted to catch the wind. The sheets and tack lines were hauled in on the lee side. The sheet ropes were released on the windward side and the tack line secured forward.

1. HALLIARDS.
2. TACK LINES.
3. SHEET LINES.
4. SHEET CAST OFF.

TACK LINES. SHEET LINES.

REEFING ~
canvas area was reduced by loosening the sheet lines and hauling on the reef lines.

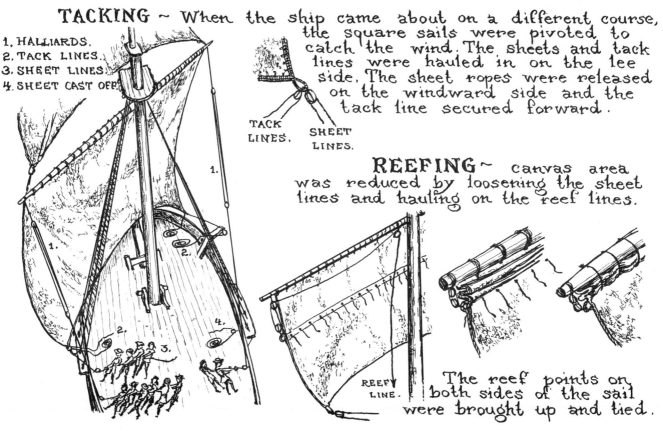

REEF LINE.

The reef points on both sides of the sail were brought up and tied.

FURLING ~

No amount of grog could coax a veteran privateersman aloft to furl the square sail until the whole was lowered the length of the lifts (1). Rightly so, for a lowered yardarm was more easily steadied, and put both the sailor and his rigging

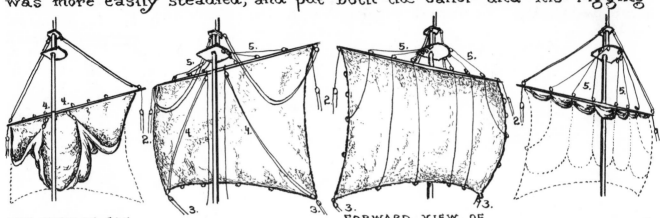

AFT VIEW OF SAIL LOWERED AND THE CORNERS (CLEWS) RAISED TO THE YARDS.

AFT VIEW OF HOISTED SAIL.

FORWARD VIEW OF HOISTED SAIL SHOWING POSITION OF BUNTLINES.

FORWARD VIEW OF LOWERED SAIL AND BUNTLINES HAULED IN.

under less strain. The wind was then spilled from the canvas by pivoting the yard until it pointed into the wind. T'was a dangerous job in high seas, for a dozen or so hands must haul around the yard's braces (2.) and others to man the sheets (3.) that ran to the sail's lower corners. The crush of a wave could sweep the deck clear of all hands, and the loose spar could smash both mast and rigging.

Once positioned, the square sail was hoisted to its yardarm by the clew lines (4.) and bunt lines (5.) The top men could scramble up the ratlines on the wind~ ward or weather side. In this approach they would be blown against - and not off- the rigging. It was a wild adventure indeed to gain a toe-hold on the foot ropes while the hull pitched and tumbled through a boiling sea. The sail was gathered in and secured by gaskets (6.) The gasket was first tied around the

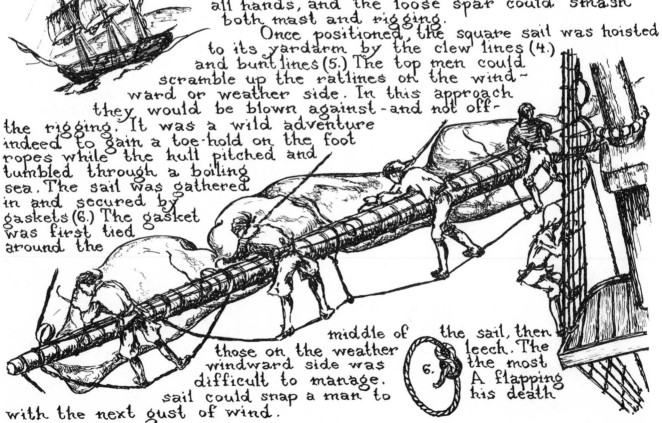

middle of the sail, then the those on the weather leech. The windward side was the most difficult to manage. A flapping sail could snap a man to his death with the next gust of wind.

SHIP OWNERS ~

A who's who of American families during the Revolution would show a sizable number investing their money in privateering. It was an entirely honorable, patriotic ~ and often profitable ~ venture. Half of all the prize monies would go to the owners. Indeed, many of these gentlemen gained in respectability as their fortunes increased ~ if one could so measure such a quality. But it was a gamble ~ make no mistake. No matter how scrappy or swift a vessel, the might of the British Navy was ranging along the coastline. If the vessel were taken, not a farthing would come from the pockets of the hard-pressed taxpayers.

With a converted merchantman or sharp new vessel nearing completion, a captain must be chosen. Family titles, friends and back-slappers stood no chance with the hard-headed Yankee businessmen. They would choose a man with a reputation for seamanship, a respected leader of his crew, a sea chest full of initiative and an incurable itch for action. Such a man would already be well-known among America's bustling seaports.

ELIAS DERBY.

DERBY WHARF, SALEM, MASSACHUSETTS. DERBY HOUSE IS TO THE RIGHT OF THE THREE EARLY 1800 STRUCTURES. THE DERBYS OWNED WHOLLY OR IN PART 25 PRIVATEERS AND HAD INTEREST IN TWICE THAT NUMBER.

COMMISSION

An application or petition must be made for a privateering commission to be granted the new captain. In the early days of the conflict, the colonial governors issued such papers ~ and Letters of Marque as well ~ by virtue of their vice-admiralty powers in time of war. By April 3rd, 1776, the Continental Congress had also begun issuing the commissions.

Generally, a captain of a privately armed ship carried both. England had made it clear that privateers would be considered as rebel pirates. Although there was no record of an American privateersman being hanged, the possibility was not appealing. Therefore the license from the Continental Congress, the voice of the new republic, was preferred as a traveling companion. On July 27th, 1780, Congress ruled that all commissions must be obtained in the office of the Secretary of Congress.

If the captain were a man of good standing, he might well have these papers stowed in his pocket in a day or two.

CAPT JOHN CARNES (1756-96) OF SALEM. HE WAS A WELL-KNOWN AND HIGHLY RESPECTED REVOLUTIONARY PRIVATEERSMAN.

INSTRUCTIONS TO PRIVATEERS

BONDS – At the time of commissioning, the owners must post a bond. This guaranteed that the captain of the vessel would follow the "Instructions" to the letter – or forfeit the amount of the bond. Congress required a substantial amount – five thousand dollars for a vessel under one hundred tons and ten thousand dollars for heavier tonnage. Earlier in the conflict, a state bond was also required. Sizable as these sums were, there was certainly no lack of petitioners. Upward to a thousand privateering vessels took to the seas during those years of conflict!

CAPTAIN ~

His word was absolute aboard his floating kingdom. Although he cared little for the rules and regulations that burdened the young Continental Navy, he expected every hand to turn to smartly at his order. The safety of his vessel depended upon it. His authority was acknowledged by a touch of a hat, and no right-thinking tar would dare crowd the distance between them to less than the length of a boathook. Discipline was the measure of smartness and efficiency aboard a fighting ship.

Yet authority without understanding could border on tyranny ~ and heaven knew the English colonies had had their fill of that! Likely the captain achieved his command after coming up through the ranks from that of a lowly cabin boy or ordinary seaman. His knowledge of the sea came from years of teamwork with his shipmates. He could appreciate a man's limitations, and worth, and thereby receive the respect of the new and veteran privateersman.

The captain must be courageous and quick-witted under the crush of an emergency. His daring could turn a potential disaster to his advantage. A much admired commander could lead a willing crew anywhere. Such a man, for example, was Hugh Hill of Beverly, Massachusetts. He was a captain one <u>had</u> to look up to, for he towered six feet six inches into the sky and weighed three hundred pounds! His privateer "Pilgrim" was the best known and most successful privateer from that port.

While visiting a tavern in L'Orient, France, a local citizen fancied himself insulted.

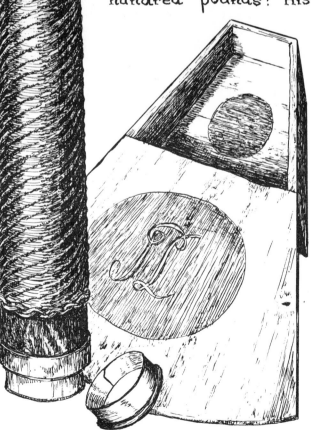

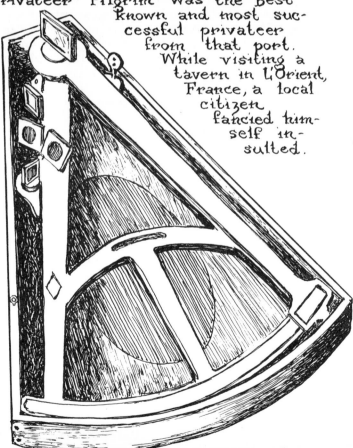

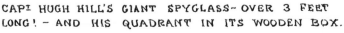

CAPT HUGH HILL'S GIANT SPYGLASS~ OVER 3 FEET LONG! ~ AND HIS QUADRANT IN ITS WOODEN BOX.

Perhaps a bit heady with wine, the Frenchman said "I will send my seconds to you in the morning!" Hill drew two pistols from his belt, held out one and bellowed "What's the matter with here and now?!" There the discussion ended.

The average privateer commander shipped aboard with his practical seamanship and Yankee intuition~ but practically no formal education in navigation. It simply wasn't available, and the few instruments of the period could be mastered with modest effort. True~ in every major port one could ferret

LIGHT SEAMAN'S CUTLASS OF THE REVOLUTION. THE ENGLISH KETLAND FLINT-LOCK NAVAL PISTOL HAS A BELT HOOK.

out a navigational school that mariner or the local instrument ive student would better spend his text rather than hear the same, re- classroom. Whatever his choice, he heavily on the time-honored method of

The captain had his orders. This business venture~ and only plump enemy were the target. If the encounter proved hasty retreat was in order. But time after time he took on the King's ships, knowing full well that there would be no cargo of value in the hold.

was instructed by a retired dealer. But the prospect- skillings on a simple cited in a makeshift would still lean dead reckoning. was a merchantmen chancy, a

Historians may never fully appreciate the quiet patriotism of these privateering captains. Yet their efforts supplied the Continental Army with more than good wishes. Captain Haraden, for example, seized no less than a thousand cannon for the American cause. With these captured arms and supplies were hundreds of enemy troops that never reached the battlefield. And some sixty of these captains took a further step and became officers in the Continental Navy. Be it private or public service, these sea-going leaders contributed handsomely to their young country.

DARK GREEN SHIP'S CHEST, OWNED BY CAPT BENJAMIN COX, 1770.

COME JOLLY FELLOWS!

And which privateer would be the choice of the volunteer? Ask this and he would answer with his own question - who's the skipper?! Few towns in Revolutionary America were more than one hundred miles from the sea, and every local newspaper made haste to announce the latest privateering exploits. Tavern talk and wagging tongues made point of the string of prizes brought in by each captain. The greater the number, the greater his reputation. It followed that the "lucky" vessel could only be as successful as its commander.

The captain chose his own crew. There was no need for drumming up recruits with a band playing stirring martial tunes, flags and the patriotic speeches. Such inducements were the practice of the thin-ranked naval service. Privateering caught the fancy of a red-blooded man with a yen for the sea. He would have less discipline and shorter cruises than in the Navy - and more jingle in his pockets if the hunt took some worthwhile prizes. There would be no wages paid to the captain or the crew in any event, but the chance for sudden riches was just over the horizon.

LANDLUBBERS - Country boys stole off during the night, leaving their distressed parents a "gone a-privateering" note. Doctors, ministers, lawyers, shopkeepers, farmers, runaway negro slaves and an occasional Indian quickly filled the requirement that one third of the crew be landsmen. They were expected to get their sea legs in short order. As part of the outsized crew (for privately armed ships were always crowded) they were needed as sailors, gunners, moving captured cargo, prisoner guards, carpenter's helpers to repair damage and as prize crews. The latter might strip the vessel down to one tenth of the able-bodied seamen aboard. This was to be expected on a successful cruise, for each prize crew was made up of between twelve to twenty men.

MARINE GUARD ~ These "Gentlemen Volunteers" were a cut above their shipmates. All hailed from highly respected and well-known families. They were naturals for the marine guard, for they were young, intelligent, well-schooled and generally excellent marksmen. As such, they acted as a police detail, enforcing the officers' orders among the crew. When approaching an enemy vessel, they took up their sharp-shooters stations. Usually they led the boarding party, then made up much of the prisoner guard. On shore raids, they could be counted upon to carry out the mission with efficiency and dispatch.

SEAMEN ~ The remaining two-thirds of the crew were salty "tars" (It was an old custom to tar one's trousers, hats and other clothing to make them waterproof). They were the privateer's veteran sailors and former fishermen - and not a one rated able seaman until his competence passed the approval of his peers. Teamwork during a sea action left no room for bumbling. Alertness and strength were obvious advantages. Height was not. The headroom below decks was rarely over five feet ten inches. Cracked skulls from low beams were headaches the captain could ill afford. Therefore shorter men were preferred. Six footers need not apply.

An occasional seaman could be found aboard who was not an American. With no need for the muscle from English press gangs, sailors aboard captured prize vessels could volunteer for a share in future profits. Yet he must have uneasy thoughts, for disloyalty to the King would gain nothing but a yardarm noose if he were recaptured. Despite this risk, there was an uncertain quality of his efforts during battle against his countrymen.

OFFICERS ~ Picked with more than the usual care by the captain, the officers came up through the ranks as an ordinary seaman. Cruel, overbearing or dull officers would guarantee a surly crew. Men confined to the cramped isolation of a ship quickly took on their officers' attitudes. Disciplined freedom, with a generous helping of understanding, went a long way toward making the cruise smooth and pleasant. The officers stations and ranks generally followed the pattern of the Navy. A sailing master was sometimes included in the roster for his navigational skills, but like as not the commander preferred to do that chore himself.

SHARES

The volunteer's share in the fortunes of his vessel were as negotiable as our present day certificates of stock. Upon signing the **ARTICLES**, a man was free to sell a part or the whole of his shares. The lad who left home without a copper, the married man with a family to support in his absence, or the seaman who had drunk his previous prize money dry could thereby obtain ready cash. Depending on the reputation of the captain, season of the year or urgency of the seller, the price could be low or very high indeed. No right-thinking privateersman, unless hard-pressed, would chose to handle his affairs in this way. Those shares might make his fortune if even a single captured enemy was burdened with a valuable cargo.

ARTICLES OF AGREEMENT,

MADE AND AGREED UPON BETWEEN CAP-
TAIN   COMMANDER OF THE
PRIVATEER   MOUNTING
CARRIAGE GUNS AND COMPANY.
(A SUMMARY OF ARTICLES TO BE SIGNED
BY SHIP'S OFFICERS AND CREW)

ARTICLE I
THE SHIP'S OWNERS SHALL PROVIDE SUFFI-
CIENT ARMS, AMMUNITION AND PROVISIONS
FOR A CRUISE EXTENDING NOT MORE
THAN   MONTHS. IN RETURN, THEY SHALL
RECEIVE HALF OF ALL PRIZES TAKEN.

ARTICLE II
THE CAPTAIN MUST, TO THE BEST OF HIS
ABILITY, CARRY OUT THE "INSTRUCTIONS".

ARTICLE III
THE OFFICERS AND CREW MUST REPORT
FOR DUTY WHEN SO ORDERED BY THE CAP-
TAIN, THEY MUST PERFORM THEIR DUTIES
TO THE BEST OF THEIR SKILL AND ABILITY.

ARTICLE IV
REWARDS AND PUNISHMENTS~

1. ANY OF THE COMPANY LOOSING AN
ARM OR LEG IN AN ENGAGEMENT, OR IS
OTHERWISE DISABLED AND UNABLE TO EARN
HIS BREAD, SHALL RECEIVE ONE THOUSAND
POUNDS FROM THE FIRST PRIZE TAKEN.

2. WHOEVER FIRST DISCOVERS A SAIL THAT
PROVES TO BE A PRIZE, SHALL RECEIVE ONE
HUNDRED POUNDS AS A REWARD FOR HIS
VIGILANCE.

3. WHOEVER ENTERS AN ENEMY SHIP AFTER
BOARDING ORDERS ARE ISSUED, SHALL RECEIVE
THREE HUNDRED POUNDS FOR HIS VALOR.

4. WHOEVER IS GUILTY OF GAMING OR
QUARRELING SHALL SUFFER SUCH PUNISHMENT
AS THE CAPTAIN AND OFFICERS SEE FIT.

5. ANY MAN, ABSENT FROM THE SHIP
FOR TWENTY FOUR HOURS WITHOUT LEAVE,
SHALL BE GUILTY OF DISOBEDIENCE; COWARD-
ICE, MUTINY, THEFT, PILFERING, EMBEZZLEMENT,
CONCEALMENT OF GOODS BELONGING TO THE
SHIP OR HER COMPANY, STRIP OR THREATEN
ANY MAN OR BEHAVE INDECENTLY TO A WOM-
AN~ SHALL LOOSE HIS SHARES AND RECEIVE
SUCH OTHER PUNISHMENT AS THE CRIME
DESERVES. SUCH FORFEITED SHARES SHALL
BE DISTRIBUTED TO THE REMAINING
SHIP'S COMPANY.

6. SEVEN DEAD SHARES SHALL BE SET
ASIDE AND DIVIDED BY THE CAPTAIN AND
OFFICERS AMONG THOSE WHO BEHAVE BEST
AND DO THE MOST FOR THE INTEREST AND
SERVICE OF THE CRUISE.

7. WHEN A PRIZE IS TAKEN AND SENT
INTO PORT, THE PRIZE MASTER AND THE MEN
ABOARD ARE RESPONSIBLE FOR WATCHING
AND UNLOADING THE PRIZE. IF ANY NEG-
LIGENCE RESULTS IN DAMAGE, THEIR SHARES
WILL BE HELD ACCOUNTABLE.

8. IF THE COMMANDER IS DISABLED, THE
NEXT HIGHEST OFFICER WILL STRICTLY COM-
PLY WITH THE RULES, ORDERS, RESTRICTIONS
AND AGREEMENTS BETWEEN THE OWNERS OF
THE PRIVATEER AND THE COMMANDER.

SHARES TO BE PROPORTIONED AS FOLLOWS~

	SHARES		SHARES
CAPTAIN	8	STEWARD	2
FIRST LIEUTENANT	4	SAILMAKER	2
SECOND LIEUTENANT	4	GUNNER'S MATE	1½
MASTER	4	BOATSWAIN'S MATE	1½
SURGEON	4	CARPENTER'S MATES	1½
OFFICER OF MARINES	2	COOPER	1½
PRIZE MASTER	2	SURGEON'S MATE	1½
CARPENTER	2	ARMORER	2
GUNNER	2	SERGEANT-MARINES	2
BOATSWAIN	2	COOK	2
MASTER'S MATES	2	GENTLEMEN VOLRS	1
CAPTAIN'S CLERKS	2	BOYS UNDER 16 YEARS	½

9. IF ANY OFFICER OR ANY OF THE
COMPANY BE TAKEN PRISONER ABOARD A
CAPTURED PRIZE VESSEL, HE SHALL RECEIVE
A SHARE IN ALL PRIZES TAKEN DURING THE
REMAINDER OF THE PRIVATEER'S CRUISE IN
THE SAME MANNER AS HE WOULD IF
ACTUALLY ABOARD. HOWEVER, HE MUST OBTAIN
HIS LIBERTY BEFORE THE END OF THE CRUISE
OR MAKE EVERY EFFORT TO JOIN THE PRI-
VATEER, OR ELSE HIS PRIZE MONEY SHALL
BE FORFEITED TO THE OWNERS AND THE
SHIP'S COMPANY.

10. THE CAPTAIN SHALL HAVE FULL POWER
TO DISPLACE ANY OFFICER WHO MAY BE
FOUND UNFIT FOR THE POST.

11. THE CAPTAIN AND HIS PRINCIPAL
OFFICERS SHALL HAVE FULL POWER TO APPOINT
AN AGENT FOR THE SHIP'S COMPANY.

12. THE CAPTAIN, LIEUTENANTS, MASTER,
SURGEON AND OFFICER OF THE MARINES
SHALL NOT BE ENTITLED TO ANY PART OF
THE DEAD SHARES.

CREW'S CLOTHING

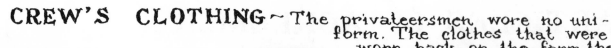

~ The privateersmen wore no uniform. The clothes that were worn back on the farm, the shop, or the fishing vessel were good enough.

1A.

1B.

1C.

1D.

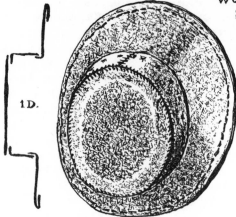

1E.

Still, it made sense to wear some of the gear that had proved useful over long years of sea use.

1. HATS~ THE CONVENTIONAL WIDE-BRIMMED HAT WAS WORN
   A. THREE-CORNERED OR COCKED.
   B. TURNED UP ALL AROUND.
   C. TURNED UP ON ONE OR BOTH SIDES.
   D. SAILOR'S FLAT-BRIMMED HAT FROM PIECE OF SHIP'S CANVAS AND WATERPROOFED WITH TAR OR PAINT.
   E. KNIT CAP.
2. BLACK (IT HID THE DIRT) NECKERCHIEF. ORIGINALLY CALLED A "SWEAT RAG", IT WAS WORN ABOUT THE NECK OR FOREHEAD.
3. PEA COAT~ SEAMAN'S TOP COAT FOR COLD WEATHER - OF "PILOT CLOTH".
4. BELL-BOTTOMED TROUSERS COULD BE EASILY ROLLED UP WHEN SCRUBBING DECKS OR WADING ASHORE.
5. QUEUES ~
   LAID UP IN -
   A. FOUR-STRAND SQUARE SINNET OR
   B. RATTAIL.
   SEA-GOING TARS FAVORED EELSKINS FOR COVERING THE QUEUE. THE SKINS WERE KEPT ABOARD IN BRINE. EACH WAS ROLLED UP AND SECURED AT THE TOP WITH RIBBON AND BOW.

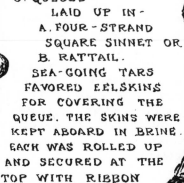

5A.   5B.

DITTY BAG ~

The sailor's small gear was stowed in this small canvas sack. It was from seven to fourteen inches in length, with a lanyard of about eighteen inches. This specimen, drawn about one fourth the actual size, belonged to Cap.ᵗ Reuben Chase. He served with John Paul Jones on the "Bon Homme Richard" in the sea fight with the "Serapis". 1779.

WROUGHT SCISSORS, DRAWN FOUR-FIFTHS SIZE.

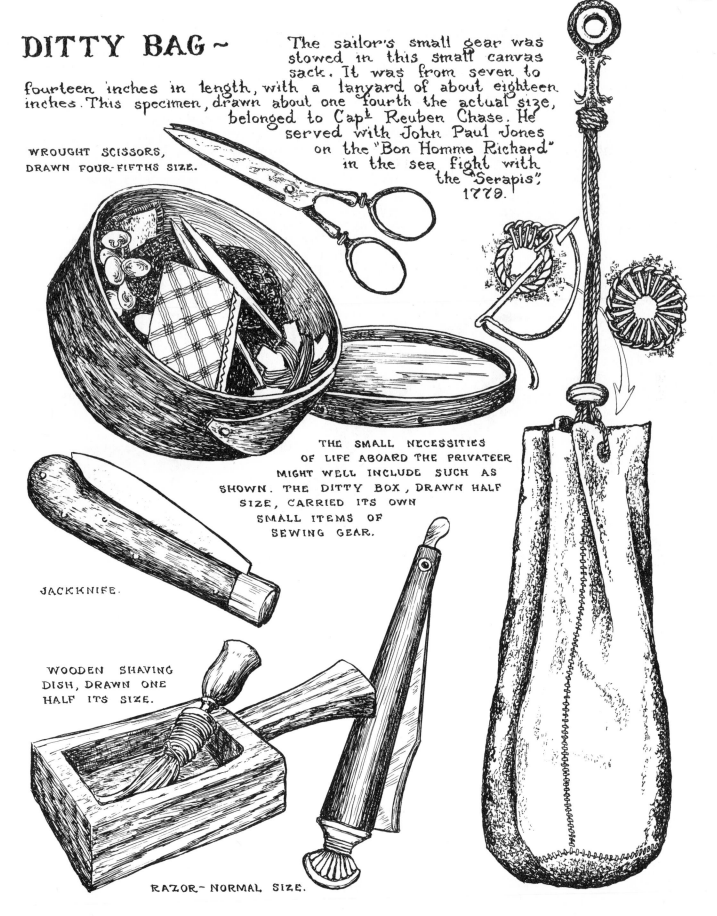

THE SMALL NECESSITIES OF LIFE ABOARD THE PRIVATEER MIGHT WELL INCLUDE SUCH AS SHOWN. THE DITTY BOX, DRAWN HALF SIZE, CARRIED ITS OWN SMALL ITEMS OF SEWING GEAR.

JACKKNIFE.

WOODEN SHAVING DISH, DRAWN ONE HALF ITS SIZE.

RAZOR — NORMAL SIZE.

SOUNDS ON SHIPBOARD

The newcomer was expected to fit into the organized confusion on shipboard before his stern collected many barnacles. The boatswain's "calls" or "pipes" shrilled above the din, much as it had back in the galley slave days of Greece and Rome when a flute marked the stroke. The privateersman had best jump to the tune~ and in the right direction! By tongue, lung or palm pressure, the variety of calls might send the crew scurrying to the tops, lifting the braces, answering the calling up of all hands, attention to orders, sounding to quarters, upping all hammocks, and a host of other commands.

Other orders were issued without any benefit of middlemen. The captain himself would shout through his speaking trumpet~ and the salty language that tumbled from its bell would flatten a landlubber's ears. Biblical references were frequent, and without the slightest hint of reverence. But one would own that the meaning was loud and clear~ no urging or pleading~ just do it, and smartly!

BO'SUN'S PIPE~ DRAWN HALF SIZE.

CAPTAIN'S SPEAKING TRUMPET~ DRAWN HALF SIZE.

QUARTERDECK

No amount of hurry should overlook the quarterdeck salute. That honored elevation at the ship's stern represented the captain's authority. Above the stern flew the young nation's flag~ a symbol of a land governed by its citizens. The captain also touched his cap to this higher power. Anyone privileged by rank or rate to be upon the quarterdeck must acknowledge this sign of respect.

The quarterdeck held a commanding view of the ship and the ocean beyond. The course and destiny of the privateer was steered from this point. Smaller vessels could be handily managed with a tiller attached directly to the rudder. Larger ships were better served by a series of blocks and tackles to a wheel. The added purchase gave a more manageable positioning of the rudder.

READY FOR SEA

Accounts of a landlubber boarding an eighteenth century armed vessel are rare indeed. However, Jacob Bailey, hailing from Rowley, Massachusetts, did just that on a blustery January in 1760. The Reverend Bailey (for such he was, having his license to preach after graduating from Harvard College) recorded a lively record of his journey as a passenger to England. The twenty-gun ship "Hind" lay at anchor, and he approached the seafaring life much as one of his privateering countrymen might have done fifteen years later.

"The wind was blowing strong and it was some time before we could get on board ship. At length, with difficulty, I clambered up the side and found myself in the midst of a most horrid confusion. The deck was crowded full of men, and the boatswain's shrill whistle, with the swearing and hallooing of the petty officers, almost stunned my ears. I could find no retreat from this dismal hubbub, but was obliged to continue jostling among the crowd above an hour before I could find anybody at leisure to direct me."

Part of the human tide that swept before Mr. Bailey's eyes was likely involved in securing the small boat that brought him aboard. The great reach of the fore and main yard spars, with their running rigging pressed into service as hoists, lifted the boat above the level of the gunwhale. Blocks and tackles, attached to the main stay, brought the boat in amidships. It was then lowered into its cradle and lashed securely.

FORE AND MAIN YARD TACKLES HOISTED BOAT.

STAY TACKLE TURNED BOAT'S BOW INBOARD. FORE YARD TACKLE SLACKED.

WEIGHT OF BOAT STERN WAS TAKEN BY AFT STAY TACKLE. THE MAIN YARD TACKLE WAS SLACKED. BOAT WAS THEN LOWERED TO THE DECK.

STAY LASHING FOR LIFTING BOAT.

FORE AND AFT OF THE BOAT WERE HEAVY SUPPORTS. SPARE SPARS WERE LASHED TO THE SUPPORTS FOR ECONOMY OF SPACE.

WEIGH ANCHOR!

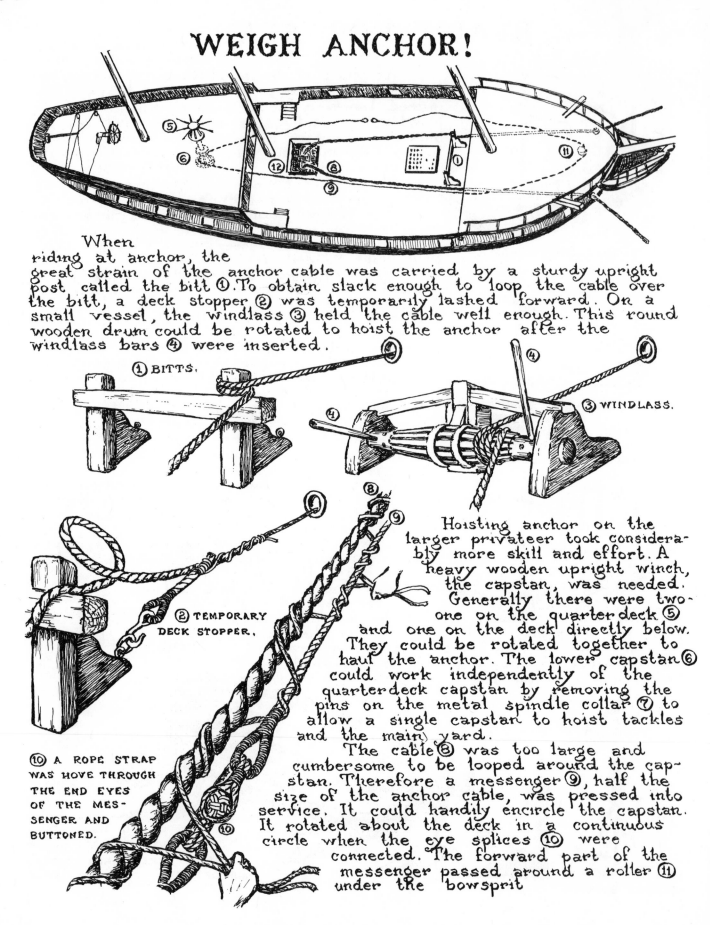

When riding at anchor, the great strain of the anchor cable was carried by a sturdy upright post called the bitt ①. To obtain slack enough to loop the cable over the bitt, a deck stopper ② was temporarily lashed forward. On a small vessel, the windlass ③ held the cable well enough. This round wooden drum could be rotated to hoist the anchor after the windlass bars ④ were inserted.

① BITTS.

③ WINDLASS.

② TEMPORARY DECK STOPPER.

⑩ A ROPE STRAP WAS HOVE THROUGH THE END EYES OF THE MESSENGER AND BUTTONED.

Hoisting anchor on the larger privateer took considerably more skill and effort. A heavy wooden upright winch, the capstan, was needed. Generally there were two—one on the quarterdeck ⑤ and one on the deck directly below. They could be rotated together to haul the anchor. The lower capstan ⑥ could work independently of the quarterdeck capstan by removing the pins on the metal spindle collar ⑦ to allow a single capstan to hoist tackles and the main yard.

The cable ⑧ was too large and cumbersome to be looped around the capstan. Therefore a messenger ⑨, half the size of the anchor cable, was pressed into service. It could handily encircle the capstan. It rotated about the deck in a continuous circle when the eye splices ⑩ were connected. The forward part of the messenger passed around a roller ⑪ under the bowsprit

EIGHT TO TEN CAPSTAN BARS, NINE FEET IN LENGTH, GAVE THIRTY TWO OR MORE MEN ROOM ENOUGH TO BEND THEIR BACKS.

THE ANCHOR WAS SIZABLE ~ FIVE HUNDRED POUNDS FOR EVERY HUNDRED TONS OF TONNAGE. STOCK WAS OF TWO PIECES OF WOOD, CLAMPED WITH IRON HOOPS. A SLIGHT BEVEL TO THE SQUARE IRON BARS WAS ALL A FORGE COULD MANAGE.

⑤

⑦ SPINDLE COLLAR.

⑥

Forward on the gun deck, the messenger was laid alongside the cable. A "nipper man" temporarily lashed a series of small ropes about the cable and the messenger. A number of "nipper boys", each holding the after end of one nipper and the forward end of the next, walked the two ropes aft. When near the cable hatch ⑫, the nippers were removed and brought forward by the boys for another lashing and another walk.

As the cable was hauled through the hawsepipes, sailors scrubbed off as much mud as possible with broom and buckets of water. None the less, minute sea life made the cable slippery and it was often necessary to sprinkle sand on the slimy surface to make the nippers hold.

THE MESSENGER TURNED WELL WITH THREE LOOPS.

PAWLS DROPPED INTO BASE NOTCHES AS THE CAPSTAN REVOLVED, PREVENTING UNWINDING.

THIS GILDED CATHEAD CARVING GLARED FROM AND GAVE GOOD LUCK TO THE FAMOUS FRIGATE CONSTITUTION OF LATER DAYS.

FISHING ~ A YARDARM TACKLE RAISED THE ANCHOR TO BE SECURED ~ FREQUENTLY TO THE CHANNEL.

CATTING THE ANCHOR ~ A ROPE WITH ITS END STOPPERED WAS PASSED THROUGH THE CATHEAD, THEN THROUGH THE ANCHOR RING TO A CLEAT ON THE CAP-HEAD. IT WAS THEN MADE FAST TO A TIMBER HEAD.

CABLE CRISIS ~ The sudden appearance of hostile sail left no time for such an orderly anchor raising. The privateersman would sooner cut his cable than be caught as a stationary target. Either the cable was abandoned or marked with a buoy for later salvage.

WATCHES

MOORING BUOY MADE FROM A PIECE OF OLD MAST.

The efficiency and ease with which a privateering vessel became sail-borne depended on a well-considered watch billet. Posted on a conspicuous bulkhead, the officers and men were divided into two watches, each volunteer assigned to whatever best suited his skills. The larboard (the "load board" or left side for loading became the "port" side in 1846) and starboard (the "steer board" dated from ancient times when the steering oar was on the right side) watches alternated every four hours. There was one fortunate exception - the dog watches. The first and second dog were two hours each, assuring the seamen that he would not serve the same stint the following day. However, getting the vessel underway required "double shifts" - that is, the off duty watch below was called up to help man the sheets and generally begin the cruise "shipshape and Bristol Fashion".

Mid-watch = midnight to 4:00 A.M.
Morning watch = 4:00 A.M. to 8:00 A.M.
Forenoon watch = 8:00 A.M to noon.
Afternoon watch = noon to 4:00 P.M.
First dog watch = 4:00 P.M. to 6:00 P.M.
Second dog watch = 6:00 P.M. to 8:00 P.M.
Night watch = 8:00 P.M. to midnight.

Anchor watch = In port, the watch was reduced to but three or four men.

HANGING HALF HOUR SAND GLASS.

SHIP'S BELL

~ It was a rare volunteer who owned an expensive pocket time piece. All time was kept by sand glasses. On the half hour, the glass was turned and the bell struck. The weary welcomed the eight bells that sent them back to their hammocks. For example, the mid-watch would sound in this way:

1 bell * 12:30 A.M.
2 bells ** 1:00 A.M.
3 bells ** * 1:30 A.M.
4 bells ** ** 2:00 A.M.
5 bells ** ** * 2:30 A.M.
6 bells ** ** ** 3:00 A.M.
7 bells ** ** ** * 3:30 A.M.
8 bells ** ** ** ** 4:00 A.M.

ON A LARGER SHIP, THE BELL HUNG IN A SMALL BELFRY AT THE AFTER EDGE OF THE FORECASTLE.

A SMALLER SHIP'S BELL IN BRACKET.

This proceedure was repeated each watch, the quartermaster striking the bell when the glass was "capsized".

ADVICE FOR TOPMEN

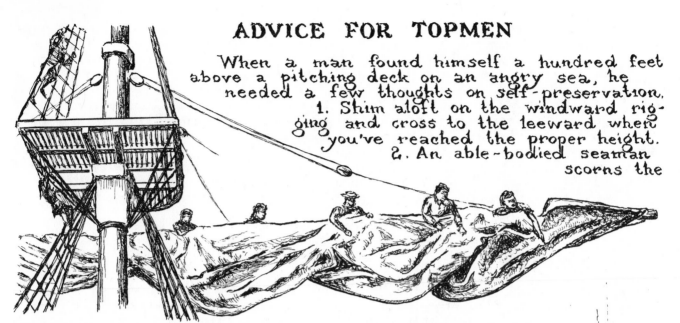

When a man found himself a hundred feet above a pitching deck on an angry sea, he needed a few thoughts on self-preservation.
1. Shin aloft on the windward rigging and cross to the leeward when you've reached the proper height.
2. An able-bodied seaman scorns the square openings in the top platform - the "lubber's hole." Instead, he climbs the ratlines to and continues on the short out-leaning shrouds to the platform.
3. Never, but never let go of one rope until another is firmly in hand. Always remember - one hand for yourself and another for the ship. A man falling overboard from aloft has little chance unless lines break his fall, and the distance to the sea is no more than forty feet.
4. If your fate is the water and you're alive enough to know it, keep cool and steady. Turn away from the wind and paddle gently. Every now and then raise your arm to direct the rescue boat. Don't waste your energy by shouting or trying to swim back to the ship. Even in high seas you can remain afloat for half an hour, time aplenty for the small boat to heave you safely aboard.
5. After your first trek to the tops, you must "pay your footing". All hands must be treated to a mug of rum.

Not all ship members were assigned to the larboard and starboard watches. There were those who carried out their duties throughout the day - the lieutenants, surgeon, sailing master, lieutenant of the marines, and the clerk. They were known as "idlers", but with the cry "All hands!" they tumbled deckside with the rest. As noted, there were the privileged who trod the hallowed boards of the quarter deck. Lesser "idlers", such as the boatswains, gunners, sailmaker, cook and carpenter kept clear of the sanctity of that region, and often referred to the quarter deck afterguard as "sea dandies" and "silk socks gentry".

BELOW DECK

The Reverend Mr. Bailey, duly impressed with the organized confusion on the deck of the ship "Hind", found his way below with the help of a knowledgable hand. "I thanked him for his kindness and readily followed him down the ladder into a dark and dismal region, where the fumes of pitch, bildge water, and other kinds of nastiness almost suffocated me in a minute. We had not proceeded far before we entered a small appartment, hung round with damp and greasy canvas, which made, on every hand, a most gloomy and frightful appearance. In the middle stood a table of pine, varnished over with nasty slime furnished with a bottle of rum and an old tin mug with a hundred and fifty bruises and several holes, through which the liquor poured in as many streams. This was quickly filled with toddy and as speedily emptied by two or three companions who presently joined us in this doleful retreat. Not all the scenes of horror about us could afford me much dismay till I received the news that this detestable appartment was allotted by the captain to be the place of my habitation during the voyage!"

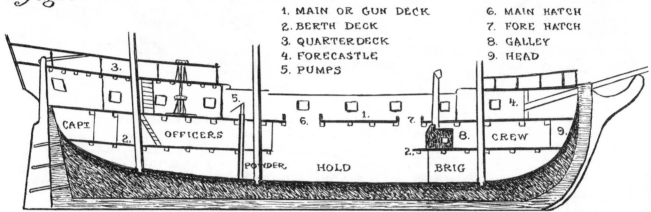

1. MAIN OR GUN DECK
2. BERTH DECK
3. QUARTERDECK
4. FORECASTLE
5. PUMPS
6. MAIN HATCH
7. FORE HATCH
8. GALLEY
9. HEAD

Mr. Bailey, it would seem, bunked down in the steerage country. Located on the port side of the berth deck, it was neither the best nor the worst of the ship's accommodations. The warrant officers~ such as the boatswain, gunnery, carpenter, steward and captain's clerk~ had a degree of privacy from the bulk of the crew. Rough hewn it was, like the rest of the privateer, but homey enough for any eighteenth century mariner.

Lanthorns, spotted at strategic points on the berth deck, did their feeble best to penetrate the gloom below deck. A lubber, with more inquisitiveness than good sense, might take a turn down the port fore-and-aft gangway and onto the parallel gangway on the opposite side. This was the officers' country, offering a temporary haven from shipboard routine. Temporary they were, for when the berth deck was also the gun deck, each compartment bulkhead could be removed. Cannon were part of the decor of these cabins. When closing in for action, down came the partitions. The cannon crew must have all the elbow room they needed.

CABIN LANTERN USED BEFORE 1750. TWO FEET HIGH, WOODEN.

WROUGHT IRON CANDLE HOLDER WITH POINT FOR STICKING INTO BEAMS.

Aft of the officers' quarters on the starboard side was the wardroom. The officers could meet, read and dine in this more spacious area. And still further aft was the ultimate in shipboard privacy ~ the captain's cabin. Here the captain could digest in peace, perhaps aided by a mug of punch. This concoction of spices and hot water, generously laced with brandy or rum, helped make a day of decisions more tolerable.

An attentive steward saw to his every want. Forward of the steerage and officers' country, flanked by the port and starboard gangways, was a great dark and dank hole. Below and on either side, large shelves of grating projected. These were the "cable tiers". The great lengths of the starboard cable was coiled and dried on the port grating, while the port cable rested on the starboard shelf. The ends of both were firmly secured to the base of the main mast to prevent losing the whole when dropping anchor. Lesser ropes were stored inside the great anchor cable coils ~ messengers, nippers, cat and fish hooks and pendant tackle.

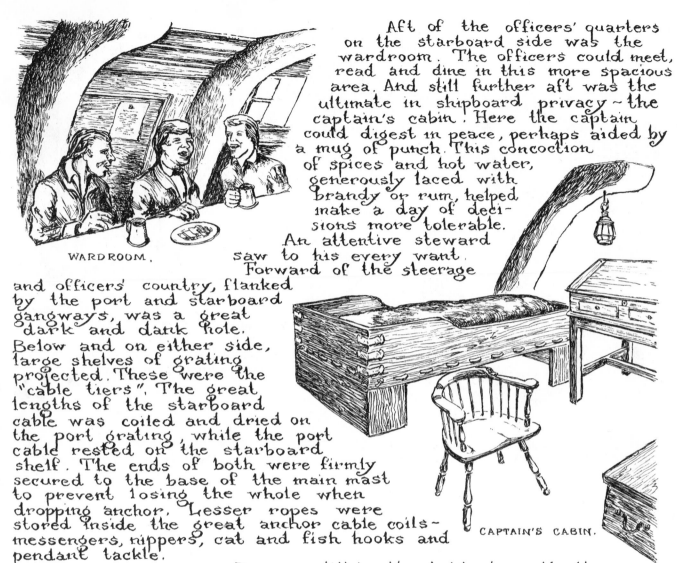

WARDROOM.

CAPTAIN'S CABIN.

PEWTER THUNDER JUG.

Deeper still in the hold, beneath the main hatchway, were stored the shot and cannon balls. This bulk of heavy iron served as ballast. Being centered, any number could be removed without sacrificing the fore-and-aft trim. The powder locker was generally built here with as much fire and water security as possible. Both ball and powder could be hoisted into action through the hatch above.

Forward in the hold, roughly between the main and forward hatches, was a more permanent ballast of stone or pig iron. Planks or dunnage (those chunks of wood, about the size used in a landlubber's fireplace) covered the ballast to keep storage above the wood layer free of bilge water. And there were casks aplenty ~ drinking water and grog ~ all stored with bungs up. On top or forward of these were the provision barrels ~ beef on the port side, pork on the starboard,

42

MEAT CASK.

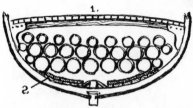

SECTION OF STOWAGE IN
HOLD AMIDSHIPS.

1. BERTH OR LOWER DECK.
2. BALLAST.
3. FORE BULKHEAD.
4. SHOT LOCKER.
5. MAINMAST.
6. PUMPS.
7. AFT BULKHEAD.

GROUND STORAGE ~ THE
FIRST LAYER ABOVE THE
BALLAST.

~The ballast and
stowage was placed
as near the center
of gravity as possible
to prevent rolling and pitching.

and flour, potatoes, rice and the like, in the wings or side.
Pieces of dunnage were used to chock the barrels to prevent
shifting in heavy seas. But privateering cruises were short, and a
full hold of provisions was unnecessary. With a
hopeful eye to the future, captured prizes
would fill the remaining space.
    Near the forward bilge was storage
of another sort ~ the prison or "brig". It
was heavily grated and
ready for the first catch
of British seamen.
    Above, on the
berth deck abaft
the mainmast was
the water-breaker
or scuttlebutt. At
this meeting place
a man could wet down his innards
and bend an ear for the latest ship's
gossip.
    The crew's quarters covered the
remainder of the berth deck forward of
the galley. Boards, hinged to the vessel's
sides, served as tables for the hungry.
The men served themselves from the galley.
The tables could be secured against the
wall when the hammocks were slung.
Every inch of space was at a premium.
These pieces of canvas were hitched

ANOTHER MEAT CASK.

PEWTER TAP~
DRAWN ⅔rd SIZE.

in hooks in the overhead deck timbers with a scant fourteen inches between head to foot like so many sardines.

Dr. Solomon Drowne was aboard the private sloop of war "Hope" in 1780. He noted in his journal his envy of the landlubber's steady mansion~ no heaving and no wind howling in the cordage. But forward in the crew's quarters, with the hammocks dancing jigs in a storm, conditions were infinitely worse. Clothes drenched during the watch had little hope of drying under the dank bedding.

The thousand and one smells below intensified when the hatch was closed to prevent shipping water.

In the bow of the ship was the "head"~ the crew's toilet.

CREW'S QUARTERS.

Its position gave reasonable ventilation.

Back on deck, the morning brought the stowing of the hammocks. Larger privateers carried the convenience of hammock nettings. Strongly secured to the rail, they solved the stowage problem of bedding about a crowded vessel. The first hammock was doubled to fit the end space. Each roll that followed was laid at a forty-five degree angle like so many packed sausages. An officer sighted along the top to be certain that the canvas ends were exactly parallel to the rail. A painted canvas cover protected the whole from weather. A trim rail meant a ship-shape vessel~ and more. The netting provided an excellent barricade against small arms fire.

HAMMOCK WAS OF HEAVY CANVAS SIX FEET LONG AND THREE FEET WIDE.

IRON BRACKETS FOR THE NETTINGS WERE GENERALLY PREFERRED OVER LONG WOODEN BOXES ATOP THE RAILING. A CANNON BALL, STRIKING THE LATTER, COULD SHOWER THE GUNNERS WITH DEADLY WOODEN SPLINTERS.

CANNON

GUN FROM THE
PRIVATEER "NANCY",
CONNECTICUT ~
CAPTAIN PHIPPS.

When land had dipped below the horizon, all hands were called to quarters. This was the first of many such drills. The ship was cleared for action. All fires - cooking and lantern - must be extinguished. The cannon crews would drill over their inaccurate iron tubes until loading and firing were second nature.

The privateer's cannon made a brave show of it along the gunwales with their red wooden carriages and blacked barrels. Theirs was the thunderous voice of the citizen ship. As sea-going armament went, their roar was not very large. A small vessel would carry four-pounders (for cannon were known by the approximate weight of it's shot) while her larger privateering sister might boast of six-pounders. A four-pounder might weigh one thousand to twelve-hundred pounds and have a five or six foot barrel.

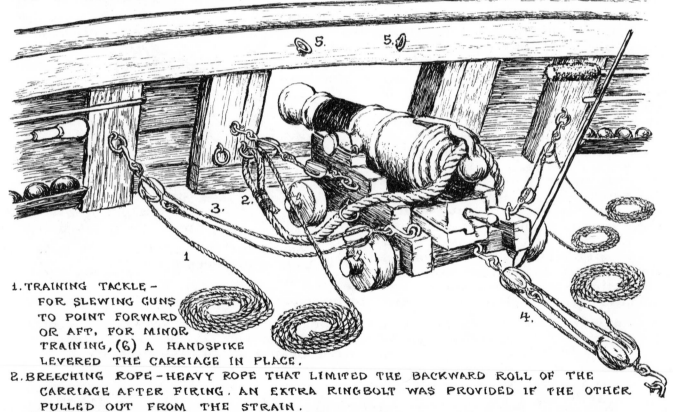

1. TRAINING TACKLE -
   FOR SLEWING GUNS
   TO POINT FORWARD
   OR AFT, FOR MINOR
   TRAINING, (6) A HANDSPIKE
   LEVERED THE CARRIAGE IN PLACE.
2. BREECHING ROPE - HEAVY ROPE THAT LIMITED THE BACKWARD ROLL OF THE
   CARRIAGE AFTER FIRING. AN EXTRA RINGBOLT WAS PROVIDED IF THE OTHER
   PULLED OUT FROM THE STRAIN.
3. SIDE TACKLE - FOR RUNNING GUN OUT WHEN READY TO FIRE.
4. TRAIN TACKLE - FOR HAULING THE GUN IN FOR LOADING.
5. TWO EYEBOLTS ABOVE GUN-PORT - MUZZLE COULD BE RAISED AND LASHED TO
   THESE TO SECURE GUN IN HEAVY WEATHER.

Weight and space occupied dictated that the privateer cannon be about two-thirds of the length of Washington's land cannon.

These were the smooth-bored long guns~and the longer the gun, the better the distance and accuracy. But theory was a far cry from actual practice. These iron monsters didn't measure up, for it was a rare gun that had its bore dead center. And "windage" or space between the ball and the bore was sizable in American and British pieces. Lacking this snug fit, the cannon ball might chatter or bounce down the length and not leave on the course hoped for. Explosion gases would surely escape around the ball and lose distance for the gunner. In a somewhat futile attempt to improve aim, a sighting notch was sometimes filed in the base ring and muzzle bell. With all its defects, the privateer's four-pounder was reasonably accurate at one hundred and fifty yards and the six-pounder at two hundred yards.

It was the practice that each gun captain and his crew come to know the idiosyncracies of their particular cannon. If it fired high or to one side, the captain would aim with that in mind. The more practice, the better the gunnery. And, just as important, was the **SPEED** of loading. The greater the hail of cannon balls toward the enemy vessel, the better the chances of scoring hits. On closing with a Britisher, a proper broadside might cripple the enemy from the outset. But a good privateer captain would then have his gunners fire their pieces at will~as soon as they could load and bring their gun to bear. A single nimble cannon crew could throw enough iron to cripple the other ship with a lucky shot.

The few foundries in the American colonies were besieged for cannon. It was their unhappy lot to have little knowledge of their manufacture, thanks to the earlier restrictions of mother England. Where the new Continental Navy waited long months for armament before they could set sail, a privately-owned vessel had scant chance of side-tracking any heavy guns. It was common practice to push off with any cannon of dubious ancestry or serviceability, then relieve the first prize taken of any better hardware. The ketch "Skunk" set sail from New Jersey with twenty men~and but two guns! Yet she took nineteen prizes, and made a handsome profit for her officers and crew.

PROJECTILES~

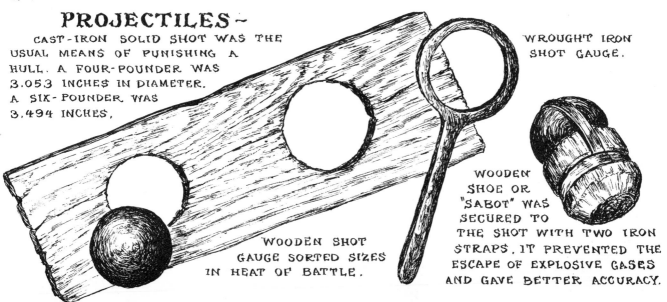

CAST-IRON SOLID SHOT WAS THE USUAL MEANS OF PUNISHING A HULL. A FOUR-POUNDER WAS 3.053 INCHES IN DIAMETER. A SIX-POUNDER WAS 3.494 INCHES.

WROUGHT IRON SHOT GAUGE.

WOODEN SHOT GAUGE SORTED SIZES IN HEAT OF BATTLE.

WOODEN SHOE OR "SABOT" WAS SECURED TO THE SHOT WITH TWO IRON STRAPS. IT PREVENTED THE ESCAPE OF EXPLOSIVE GASES AND GAVE BETTER ACCURACY.

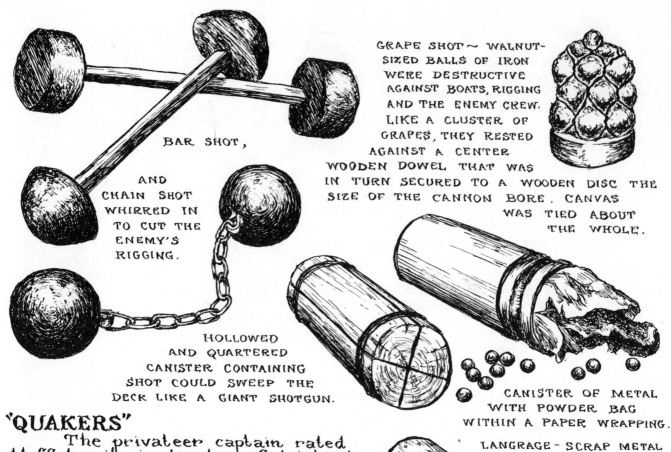

BAR SHOT,

AND CHAIN SHOT WHIRRED IN TO CUT THE ENEMY'S RIGGING.

GRAPE SHOT ~ WALNUT-SIZED BALLS OF IRON WERE DESTRUCTIVE AGAINST BOATS, RIGGING AND THE ENEMY CREW. LIKE A CLUSTER OF GRAPES, THEY RESTED AGAINST A CENTER WOODEN DOWEL THAT WAS IN TURN SECURED TO A WOODEN DISC THE SIZE OF THE CANNON BORE. CANVAS WAS TIED ABOUT THE WHOLE.

HOLLOWED AND QUARTERED CANISTER CONTAINING SHOT COULD SWEEP THE DECK LIKE A GIANT SHOTGUN.

CANISTER OF METAL WITH POWDER BAG WITHIN A PAPER WRAPPING.

LANGRAGE - SCRAP METAL PIECES COULD CHEW UP ROPES AND CAN-VAS WHEN FIRED AT THE TOPSIDE.

"QUAKERS"

The privateer captain rated bluff heavily in his bag of tricks. A prospective prize vessel would have second thoughts of resistance if a vessel bore down with her deck bristling with cannon and a boarding party howling like banshees. Too late, their captain would find much of the armament wooden! These were popularly known as Quakers - and these peaceful replicas were turned out of logs and blackened to look like the real thing. The sale of the snow "Happy Return" in Boston March 18th, 1780 put the price of each of these wooden guns at £12. In contrast, a pair of four-pound cannon went for £2500. It was an inexpensive second-best.

In 1779, the Scottish foundries of Carron produced a remarkable cannon. Called the carronade, the British privateers, as well as the King's navy, were quick to see its advantages. Briefly, it threw a shot of great size from a stubby barrel. In the usual close combat conditions at sea, the small charge of powder needed meant less bulk of iron casing to withstand the explosion. And the bore itself, not being lengthy, could better snug a ball. Less windage gave better accuracy. Britishers with such crushers as these - some larger men-of-war shot a ball weighing as much as sixty-eight pounds! - had a real edge over the Yankee privateer. He must rely on his wits and his seamanship, for by early in 1781 most British privateers were so armed. But one American armed private vessel is known to have one or more on board during the Revolution~ and these likely from a captured prize.

INSTRUCTIONS FOR GUNNERS~

1. Cast off lashings. (When action unlikely, gun is secured to eyebolts above gunport.)

2. Powder monkeys hoist powder and shot up at main hatch from the shot locker. (Small tackles~ whips~ of a single rope in a block does the job.)

3. Haul gun inboard with train tackle.

4. Remove tampion from muzzle of your gun.

5. Raise gun-port.

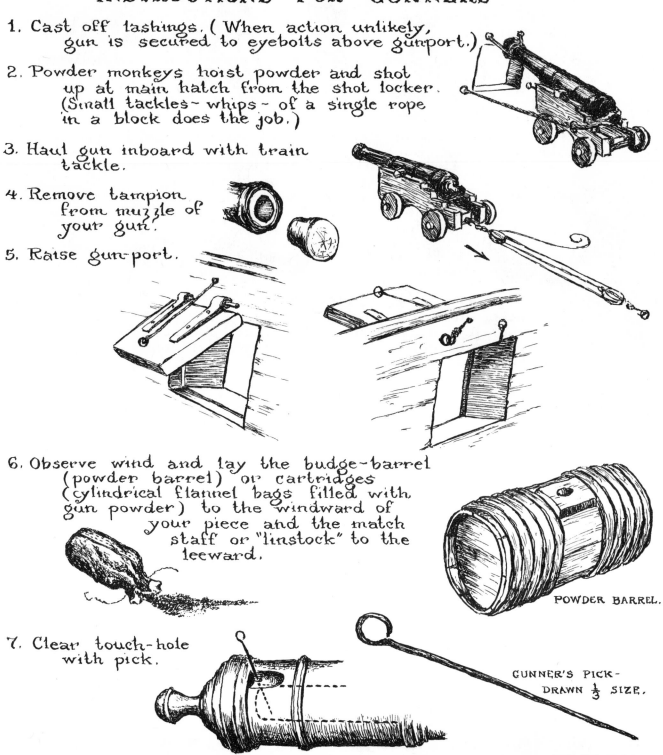

6. Observe wind and lay the budge-barrel (powder barrel) or cartridges (cylindrical flannel bags filled with gun powder) to the windward of your piece and the match staff or "linstock" to the leeward.

POWDER BARREL.

7. Clear touch-hole with pick.

GUNNER'S PICK-
DRAWN $\frac{1}{3}$ SIZE.

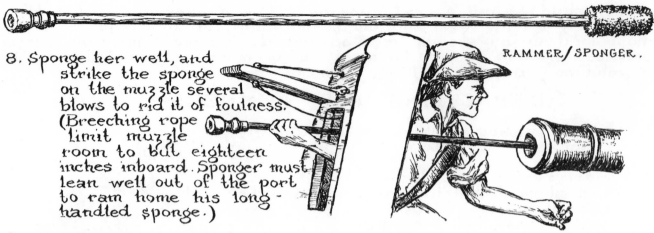

RAMMER/SPONGER.

8. Sponge her well, and
   strike the sponge
   on the muzzle several
   blows to rid it of foulness.
   (Breeching rope
   limit muzzle
   room to but eighteen
   inches inboard. Sponger must
   lean well out of the port
   to ram home his long-
   handled sponge.)

9. Stand to the right side of the gun and ram powder cartridge down
   full length of the bore. Or, if powder ladle is used instead,
   have the powder barrel held aslope. Thrust
   in your ladle, give it a shog, then
   strike off heaped powder. Put
   your ladle home in
   the chamber.
   Turn the ladle
   staff until your
   thumbs be under
   it, and give a
   sturdy shake to clear
   the powder off the ladle.
   Draw it out, keeping an upward pressure so that no
   powder is removed. Ram the powder home quietly to
   pack and make the powder fire the better, put home
   a good wad with two or three strokes. Your assistant
   should have his thumb on the touch-hole all the while.

GUNNER'S
COPPER KNIFE WOULD
NOT STRIKE A SPARK WHEN
USED AROUND GUNPOWDER.
DRAWN $\frac{1}{4}$th NORMAL SIZE.

COPPER POWDER MEASURE,
USED TO LOAD CARTRIDGES.
DRAWN $\frac{1}{2}$ SIZE.

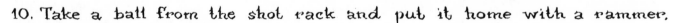

10. Take a ball from the shot rack and put it home with a rammer.

11. Follow it with a good wad of rope yarn rammed home so that no
    space be between the powder, the first wad, the shot and the
    last wad.

12. Stand to windward and prime the touch-hole with fine powder,
    letting it fill the base ring. If a cartridge is used
    first prick it open so that the priming will set off
    the charge.

POWDER CHARGE.

CARTRIDGE.

13. Run your carriage forward with the side tackle. The muzzle will project well beyond the gun port to prevent fire taking hold of the dry ship's timbers. Train tackle will prevent the carriage from rolling too far forward.

14. Aim your gun

To aim up or down, lever your handspike against a carriage step, and heave up the weighty barrel breech. The quoin— that wooden wedge with side elevation markings—is slid forward on its bed to the estimated elevation or depression.

QUOIN ON ITS BED.

To train your gun fore and aft, haul on either your right or left training tackles to slew the rear of the carriage about. A handspike will help ease the gun into position.

15. Take up your linstock and blow on the slow-match to raise a spark. Standing to the right, touch the powder in the base ring and not the touch-hole, for the upward flame would otherwise douse your slow-match. The explosion in the chamber should be instantaneous. While the ball seeks its mark, the force will drive the cannon carriage backward. The heavy breeching rope will stop its motion.

LINSTOCK.

16. Swab out the bore with your wet sheepskin sponge to extinguish any sparks before reloading. A good crew will load and fire in less than a minute.

WORMING IRON— REMOVED CHARGES FROM BARREL.

SWIVEL GUNS ~ Although not listed as part of the vessel's armament, it would be difficult to imagine a privateer not carrying its share of swivels. These were miniature cannon, many having a straight or curved wooden grip attached to the breech for ease in aiming. The oar-like type of support was in the deck rails or on stocks—vertical posts attached outside the rails. When mounted on the elevated poop and quarterdeck, they

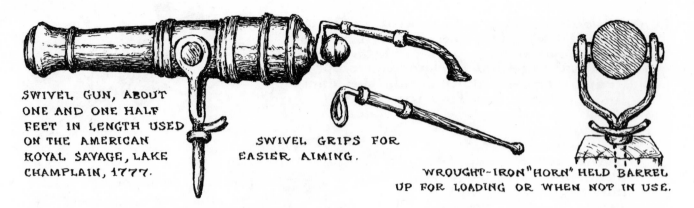

SWIVEL GUN, ABOUT ONE AND ONE HALF FEET IN LENGTH USED ON THE AMERICAN ROYAL SAVAGE, LAKE CHAMPLAIN, 1777.

SWIVEL GRIPS FOR EASIER AIMING.

WROUGHT-IRON "HORN" HELD BARREL UP FOR LOADING OR WHEN NOT IN USE.

gave a commanding sweep of the enemy topsides. Some were mounted in the crow's nest for an even better vantage point.

Most favored by the privateersmen were those swivel guns that ranged from a twenty-eight inch length with a one to one and one-half inch bore to a length of thirty-six inches with a one and one half to one and three quarter inch bore. A handful of musket balls could effectively spray a shot-gun-like blast at the Britishers.

VICTUALS

British Naval Regulations of 1790 noted that "Also every gunner ought to know that it is a wholesome thing for him to eat and drink a little meat before he doth discharge any piece of artillery, because the fumes of saltpetre and brimstone will otherwise be hurtful to his brain, so it is very hurtful to him to shoot in any piece of ordnance while his stomach is full."

If an American gun crew was inclined to follow such advice, a tolerable appetite must have grown by the time a workout on the iron tubes was through. He could look forward to a "Bill of Fair" such as was found in the log of the Salem privateer ship "Porus".

"Sunday : Beef & Pudden
Monday : Pork & Pease
Wednesday : Beef
Thursday : Beef
Friday : Pork & Beans
Saturday : Salt Fish"

Although the victualling sheet was subject to the orders of the ship's owners, the daily allowance likely followed that of the Massachusetts state navy orders of October 12, 1776 ~ one pound of bread, one pound of pork or beef, one gill of rice, and one gill of rum. A half pint of peas or beans, or one pound of potatoes or turnip might be substituted for the rice. Three quarters of a pound of butter and one half pint of vinegar were allowed weekly.

The necessity of preserving meats in brine soon snuffed out any resemblance to home cooking. The finest side of beef became a soggy, leathery mess of fibers. "Salt Junk" it was called, for "junk" was an old rope. The similarity needed no elaboration for those with timid stomachs. Of course, the brine must first be removed by a thorough watering in a "steep-tub" before boiling.

The ship's cook could redeem himself by a frequent offering

of lobscouse. Dried potato slices resembling wood chips, and soaked salt beef were hashed together. Dried peas and beans, both more likely ammunition for a musket, and pieces of unyielding hard tack were often added to the mush and cooked well. And from these unlikely ingredients came a meal that no mariner could resist.

The makings for the last-mentioned hard tack (or, if one wished, he could use the less realistic name of sea biscuit or ship's bread) were as unappetizing as the result.

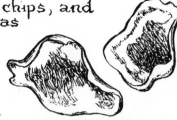

DRIED POTATOES FOR A LONG VOYAGE.

SPECIMEN OF HARD TACK, BAKED IN 1785.

~HARD TACK~

MIX ONE TEASPOON OF SALT WITH ONE POUND OF FLOUR. SHIP ENOUGH WATER TO MAKE A VERY STIFF DOUGH. CUT THE WHOLE INTO FOUR INCH SECTIONS AND PUNCH IT WITH HOLES. BAKE IN A FLAT PAN AT 250° FOR TWO OR THREE HOURS.

And now "Jolly Fellows" - your ration of grog! Each officer and man alike received one gill of rum daily - that is, a quarter of a pint. The seaman could look forward to his "nooner" - for it was time for his first drink when the sun was over the fore yard or yardarm. To take a drink was to "wet your whistle". Becoming drunk was to have "a sheet to the wind", while becoming very drunk was "three sheets to the wind". These classifications were reserved for shore leave, for a giddy topman had no place aboard a privateer. The watered offering would warm a man's innards but not dull his mind.

The British navy happily downed a similar rum ration, and it was known as "Nelson's blood" after the battle of Cape Trafalgar in 1805. The later-day hero, Admiral Horatio Nelson, gave his life in exchange for the crushing defeat of the French and Spanish fleets. Embalming was unknown, and his body was preserved in a keg of rum on the voyage back to England.

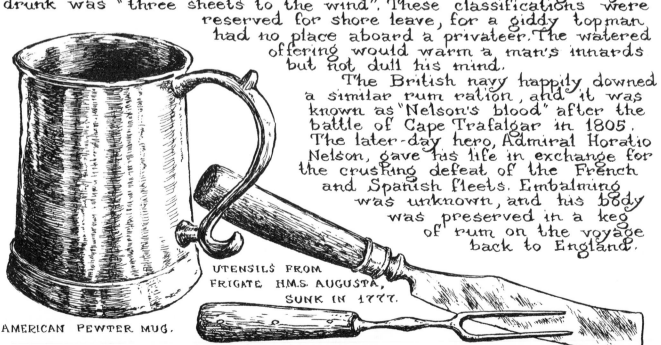

UTENSILS FROM FRIGATE H.M.S. AUGUSTA, SUNK IN 1777.

AMERICAN PEWTER MUG.

SPARE TIME

"SMALL STUFF" WAS IN PLENTY ABOARD THE PRIVATEER. SPARE MINUTES COULD TURN A TIRED PIECE OF CORDAGE INTO A HANDSOME DECORATION. ONE EXAMPLE, THE "WHIP STITCH" (LATER CALLED COACH-WHIPPING) WAS FAVORED.

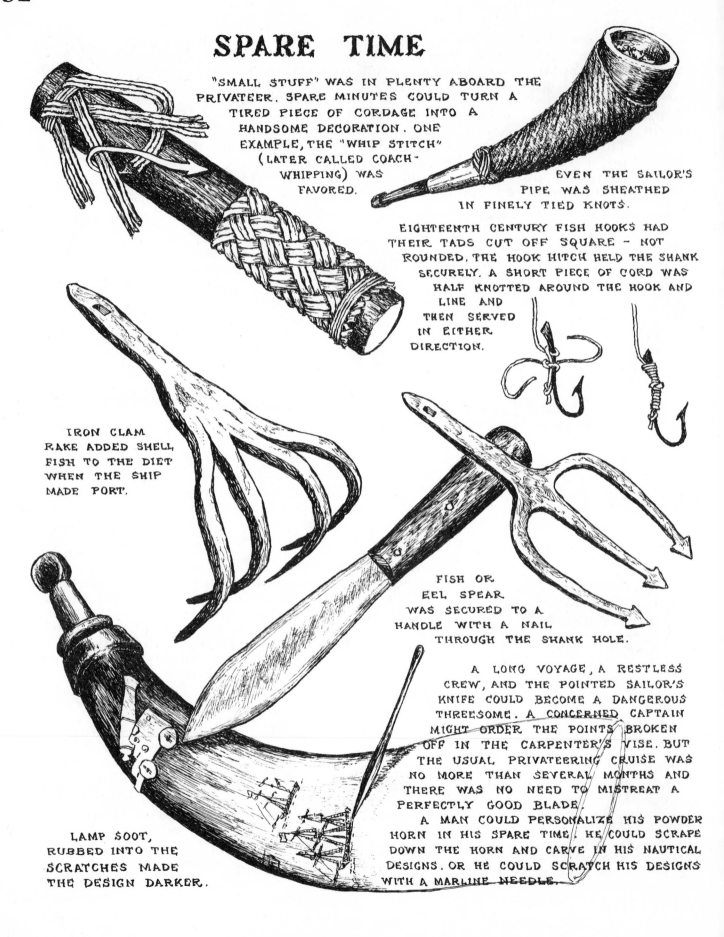

EVEN THE SAILOR'S PIPE WAS SHEATHED IN FINELY TIED KNOTS.

EIGHTEENTH CENTURY FISH HOOKS HAD THEIR TADS CUT OFF SQUARE — NOT ROUNDED. THE HOOK HITCH HELD THE SHANK SECURELY. A SHORT PIECE OF CORD WAS HALF KNOTTED AROUND THE HOOK AND LINE AND THEN SERVED IN EITHER DIRECTION.

IRON CLAM RAKE ADDED SHELL FISH TO THE DIET WHEN THE SHIP MADE PORT.

FISH OR EEL SPEAR WAS SECURED TO A HANDLE WITH A NAIL THROUGH THE SHANK HOLE.

A LONG VOYAGE, A RESTLESS CREW, AND THE POINTED SAILOR'S KNIFE COULD BECOME A DANGEROUS THREESOME. A CONCERNED CAPTAIN MIGHT ORDER THE POINTS BROKEN OFF IN THE CARPENTER'S VISE. BUT THE USUAL PRIVATEERING CRUISE WAS NO MORE THAN SEVERAL MONTHS AND THERE WAS NO NEED TO MISTREAT A PERFECTLY GOOD BLADE.

A MAN COULD PERSONALIZE HIS POWDER HORN IN HIS SPARE TIME. HE COULD SCRAPE DOWN THE HORN AND CARVE IN HIS NAUTICAL DESIGNS. OR HE COULD SCRATCH HIS DESIGNS WITH A MARLINE NEEDLE.

LAMP SOOT, RUBBED INTO THE SCRATCHES MADE THE DESIGN DARKER.

PRIVATEERING SONGS

The home folk sang the praises of their sea-faring men with such as this 1776 broadside.

Songs of another sort ~ working songs ~ were part of shipboard life. The rhythm needed for an efficient team effort made the chantey (pronounced "shanty") a natural work-mate. The chanteyman, usually a leader among the forecastle hands, sang one or more lines alone. He could improvise on the old and favorite songs, and his ingenuity could make the chorus all the more enthusiastic. The sailors' chorus, by contrast, was invariably the same and was repeated each time without change.

The song was designed for the purpose. Pulling songs had a single aim ~ to have all hands haul the halyard and sheet ropes at the same moment. Pulling songs had but one chorus.

Single-pull chanties called for one great effort, followed by a breathing spell before the next pull. The pull came on the last syllable, then the solo and the chorus repeated until the chore was done.

SOLO: WE'LL HAUL THE BOWLINE SO EARLY IN THE MORNING.
CHORUS: WE'LL HAUL THE BOWLINE, THE BOWLINE **HAUL!**

Double-pull chanties ~ for the long pulls. All hands pulled twice on each chorus.

SOLO: A YANKEE SHIP CAME DOWN THE RIVER,
CHORUS: **BLOW**, BOYS, **BLOW**.
SOLO: AND ALL HER SAILS THEY SHONE LIKE SILVER,
CHORUS: **BLOW**, MY BULLY BOYS, **BLOW**.

Another double-pull chantey is well-known in twentieth century song books ~ "Blow the Man Down".

MANLY
A FAVORITE NEW SONG,
In the AMERICAN FLEET.
Most humbly Addressed to all the JOLLY TARS who are fighting for the RIGHTS and LIBERTIES of AMERICA.
By a SAILOR.—It may be sung to the Tune of WASHINGTON.

BRAVE MANLY he is stout, and, his Men have proved true,
By taking of those English Ships, he makes their Jacks to rue;
To our Ports he sends their Ships and Men, let's give a hearty Cheer
To Him and all those valiant Souls who go in Privateers.
And a Privateering we will go, my Boys, my Boys,
And a Privateering we will go.

O all ye gallant Sailor Lads, do n't never be dismay'd,
Nor let your Foes in Battle ne'er think you are afraid,
Those dastard Sons shall tremble when our Cannon they do roar,
We'll take, or sink, or burn them all, or them we'll drive on Shore;
And a Privateering we will go, &c.

Our Heroes they're not daunted when Cannon Balls do fly,
For we're resolv'd to conquer, or bravely we will die;
Then rouse all you New-England Oaks, give MANLY now a Cheer,
Likewise those Sons of Thunder who go in Privateers.
And a Privateering we will go, &c.

Their little petty Pirates our Coast shall ne'er infest,
We'll catch their sturdy Ships, Boys, for those we do like best;
Then enter now my hearty Lads, the War is just begun,
To make our Fortunes at their Cost, we'll take them as they run.
And a Privateering we will go, &c.

While Shuldham he is flying from WASHINGTON's strong Lines,
Their Troops and Sailors run for fear, and leave their Stores behind;
Then rouse up, all our Heroes, give MANLY now a Cheer,
Here's a Health to hardy Sons of Mars who go in Privateers.
And a Privateering we will go, &c.

They talk of Sixty Ships, Lads, to scourge our free-born Land,
If they send out Six Hundred, we'll bravely them withstand;
Resolve we thus to conquer, Boys, or bravely we will die,
In fighting for our Wives and Babes, as well as LIBERTY.
And a Privateering we will go, &c.

While HOPKINS he is triming them upon the Southern Shore,
We'll scour our Northern Coast, Boys, as soon as they come o'er;
Then rouse up, all my Hearties, give Sailor Lads a Cheer,
Brave MANLY, HOPKINS, and those Tars who go in Privateers.
And a Privateering we will go, &c.

I pray you Landsmen enter, you'll find such charming Fun,
When to our Ports by Dozens their largest Ships they come;
Then make your Fortunes now, my Lads, before it is too late,
Defend, defend, I say defend an INDEPENDENT STATE.
And a Privateering we will go, &c.

While the Surf it is tossing and Cannon Balls do fly,
We surely will our Foes subdue, or cheerfully will die,
Then rouse, all you bold Seamen, brave MANLY's COMMODORE,
Should we meet with our desp'rate Foes, bless us, they will be tore.
And a Privateering we will go, &c.

Then cheer up, all my hearty Souls, to Glory let us run,
Where Cannon Balls do rattle, with sounding of the Drum;
For who would Cowards prove, or even stoop to Fear,
When MANLY he commands us in our bold PRIVATEER.
And a Privateering we will go, &c.

SALEM: Printed and Sold by the Upper End of

Windlass or capstan chanties had quite a different purpose than the pulling songs. Long and lasting efforts such as hoisting the anchor or working the pumps, required a longer and more elaborate chantey. There were always two choruses.

SOLO: OLD STORMY HE WAS A BULLY OLD MAN,
CHORUS: TO ME WAY YOU STORM ALONG.
SOLO: OLD STORMY HE WAS A BULLY OLD MAN,
CHORUS: FI-I-I, MASSA, STORM ALONG.

SUPERSTITIONS

What honest seaman could deny the mysterious fates that could befall a ship at sea? It was prudent that the privateering vessel, from its very beginning in the shipyard, be protected from whatever evil spirits that might be waiting in that vast expanse of ocean. A piece of stolen wood, mortised into the keel, was said to make a fast sailer before the wind and quick to respond to the helm. A silver coin under the mainmast step insured a successful voyage and a harbor choked with prizes. Launching ceremonies might include flowers and toppings of leaves as a throwback from ancient purification rites. The "builder's feast" in the mold loft was given as a traditional toast to the gods.

For every accident or misadventure at sea, a sailor could bring to mind some sort of forewarning gone unheeded. The new volunteer might think it nonsense, but he'd best not hand anything through the open steps of a ladder or knock a swab or bucket overboard. Opening a hatch and then turning the cover over could invite a hold full of sea water.

Coaxing up a wind to favor a becalmed ship could be handily accomplished by sticking a pocket knife into a mast, tossing a coin overboard, or having all the boys aboard whistle in unison. But should a landsman pucker up a whistle, or ANY of the ship's crew whistle when the ship had headway, a gale would soon be tearing at the rigging. A big blow was also predictable when a black cat frolicked, for it was said that it carried a gale in its tail. One further thought on wind ~ if a sailor were to spit into it, he had not long to wait before his folly caught up with him.

TWELVE FEET LONG AND CARVED OF TEAK, THE ENGLISH "BEAST" RULED THE HIGH SEAS.

FIGUREHEADS ~ A ship was a
living thing, and the early Egyptians provided her with painted eyes in the bow to see where she was going. (The hawse-holes of later vessels carried on that tradition.) These ancient decorations gave birth to the figurehead, designed to strike fear into enemy hearts, glorify a famous person, or appease the storm gods. Of all the carvings on eighteenth century British bows, the lion was a favorite. Every first rate ship carried "the beast", heavily gilded. French and English frigates often bore classical names ~ and the figure of that particular

THE FIGUREHEAD IS BELIEVED TO BE FROM THE PRIVATEER BRIGANTINE "JOLLY TAR" FROM NORFOLK, VIRGINIA, BUILT IN 1781.

god or goddess, while other vessels carried carvings of important countrymen.

There could be no mistaking the H.M.S. "Royal George" for the likeness of King George II led the way from his forward perch. The brush with the French fleet in the channel in 1778 was unfortunate for the British. The "Royal George" presented her stern and made for home. A bos'n hurriedly wound a canvas hammock about the carved head to spare the King the humility of witnessing a retreat.

To every seaman, the figurehead was the spirit of the vessel, and held in the highest regard. It was a grave omen, indeed, when it received injury.

The Yankee privateer owners were a frugal lot, not inclined to fancy up their swift-sailing vessels. But sea traditions and superstitions were not to be taken lightly. Precise drawings by the British Admiralty of captured American privateers show that most carried handsome and colorful figureheads. The sparse privateering logs and prize listings give little further information; but, safe to say, many private ships of war had their carved figures to keep a watchful eye ahead.

RELIGION

It would seem inconsistent that a God-fearing man could harbor such myths. A belief in God should give a man a freedom from fear, but it was that fear of the unknown sea perils that made him superstitious. Yet the opposites were as much at home on shipboard as the north and south of a compass. It would be a rare seaman who did not have a small, well-thumbed Bible in his ditty bag.

There were a few captains who stressed biblical names and devilishly warm places only when shouting orders through a speaking trumpet. A tolerable number, however, insisted on morning devotions at eight bells. And one captain gave the following prayer when he called his crew to quarters:

"Oh, all-sufficient Fountain and Lord of Light,
Without whose gracious and constant sprite
No labours prosper, howsoever begun,

But fly like mists before the morning sun:
Oh, raise our thoughts and clear our apprehension,
Pour down thy spirit on our weak invention;
Be thou the load-star of our wandering minds,
New rigged and bound upon new designs:
Oh, fill our canvass with a prosperous wind,
Grant that of thee we may assistance find;
So bless our talents with a fruitful loan,
That they at least return thee two for one."

COLORS AND SIGNALS

In 1782, the sloop "Lively" of Nantucket was captured while sailing under Dutch colors. On board was found "American colours, being her proper colours."

Captain William Stewart of Connecticut, commanding the privateer sloop "Porcupine", was recorded as capturing the British sloop "Fanny". It was noted that he raised colors of "a white Jack with a red Cross in it and when he came alongside he lowered that and hoisted a Continental pendant."

Out of Jamaica sailed the English privateer "St. Mary's Packet" in company with the brig "Sir George Collier". Approaching the American sloop "St. George", the former vessel pretended to be the American "General Gates" while the latter passed herself off as a tender. The "St. George was lying at anchor under British colors, while the British vessels approached"....both of them having those Colours hoisted which are used by the Congress of the United States of America." By further bluff the Yankee was seized and condemned as a prize in 1779.

Confusing? Not to a privateersman of any nation! Most vessels carried a trunkful of national flags, and used whatever seemed appropriate at the moment. It was all part of the "ruse de guerre" of privateering. Only a pudding-headed fool would advertise his real identity. No one would believe anything until the cannon balls flew. Keep 'em guessing!

This is not to say that the privateering vessel did not "show her colors". When within hailing distance, the captain might use his speaking trumpet to demand surrender. Refusal or any hostile motions would be answered by a broad-side. At that point of no return, both vessels hoisted their proper colors. When the battle was decided, the defeated would "strike her colors to end the action.

PRIVATEERS AND MERCHANTMEN FLEW THIS THIRTEEN STRIPED FLAG.

ENEMY MERCHANTMEN FLEW THE RED ENSIGN.

Occasionally the false flag trick backfired. There were instances when two Yankee vessels fled from each other, sometimes jettisoning precious cannon to make a faster retreat. And there were times when two Americans threw iron at each other before friend could be distinguished from foe. The lack of any general signal code or overall coodination between ships was one of the great flaws of the privateering venture. The independent spirits aboard these privately owned vessels accepted this lack of efficiency philosophically ~ lone-wolfing on the high seas was more to their liking.

There were times when a group of privateers banded together and hunted as a pack. Strength of numbers replaced individual daring. A code of signals was then a necessity. Such a code was discovered on the Charleston schooner "Cassandra" when captured by the H.M.S. "Bristol" in 1780. The "Cassandra" had been working with other American privateers ~ the ship "Marquis", the brigs "Trooper", "Adventure", "Randolph", and "Betsey", and the schooner "Vengeance" and "Young Neptune".

" To Sail upon a Wind ~ A Continental
Jack at Main or Mizin Peak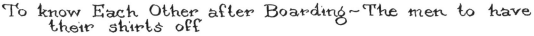

To Sail Large ~ A Pendant at
Maintopgallantmasthead

To Chase ~ A Pendant at Foretopgallant-
masthead and hoist an English Ensign
at Ensign staff

To Leave off Chase ~ Haul down the
English Ensign and pendant and
shorten sail

To Engage ~ Haul down the English Ensign and
hoist a Continental One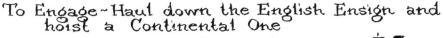

To Board ~ Hoist a Pendant at
Ensign Staff and Board
Amediately

To know Each Other after Boarding ~ The men to have
their shirts off

To Separate at the Approach of a Superior
Enomy ~ An Ensign at the Main or
Mizin Topgallant

To Know Each Other ~ The Enquirer Shall give 6 flashes
to be answered by One ~ the Ship who hails shall
ask What Ship ~ the Hailed shall Answer Mountholly ~
then the other shall reply Samboy

For Discovering a Strange Sail ~ Hoist a light
at the Ensign staff and lower it three
times distinctly

If the Enomy is thought Superior and is Necessary to
separate ~ three flashes not to be answerd

If Eaqual or Inferior ~ the divers ships Continue Chase

58

making False Fires

To Know Each Other if Attack'd ~ Each Vessel Shall hang a lanthorn over her off bow and Quarter and Keep them their during the Action ...."

These seven privateersmen, working closely with one another, were much the exception. Two or three would be more likely. As a rule, however, they would a sight rather go it alone. On May 21, 1777, the Continental frigates "Hancock" and "Boston" sailed from Boston with nine privateers. The cruise had all the elements for success, for the captains of the privately armed ships were given the same authority as regular officers, and their vessels were insured against injury by the state. It took but six days after sailing for eight of the nine privateers to sheer off from the squadron and go about their own adventures!

KNOW THE ENEMY!

The privateersman, seeking out the plump merchantman, was well aware of her quarry's habits. They had two ways of going to sea.

CONVOY ~ Often one hundred and sometimes as many as six hundred merchantmen would sail under the protection of English warships. Collecting such a number of vessels took such time and effort that word had reached sharp Yankee ears before the mass of ships had weighed anchor.

The formation was predictable. The vanship of a large fleet ~ a powerful ship of the line commanded by no lesser rank than admiral ~ led her brood like a mother duck. She would hoist signals, frequently for the faster vessels to shorten sail to let the dull sailors catch up to the rest. Sloops and brigs of war, doing guard duty on the flanks, also did service by towing laggards up to the others. Nightfall was a particularly dangerous time for the convoy, and at the "close order" signal all merchantmen would cluster as close to the vanship's stern as possible.

Here, cooperation between several privateering vessels paid off. While one enticed a guardship away, the other would cut out a laggard. The prize crew would then board and sheer her off to leeward with a zig-zag course. Once the privateersmen and the prize had scattered, the guardships had little enthusiasm to chase and leave the flanks of the fleet unprotected. Darkness, fog or foul weather worked to the privateer's advantage. Merchantmen could become scattered and fall easy prey.

SWIFT-SAILING MERCHANTMEN ~ Not all cargo-carrying ships were floating tubs with sails a-top. Some had faster lines, could crowd more canvas, and carried cannon and crew enough to take their chances alone. These lone sailers usually carried goods of considerable worth, and so were eagerly sought by the Yankee captains. One could count on a smart exchange of iron before a prize crew could secure the vessel for their own.

POSITION AT SEA

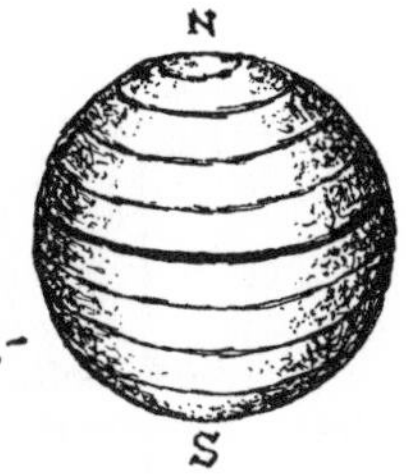

LATITUDE~ The equator encircles the earth like a stout man's belt. Parallel to this line, as gradually decreasing circles approaching the North and South Poles, are the latitudes. The specific latitude of a ship is determined by its distance from the equator. This arc (meridian) that lies between the two is part of a great circle that passes through both Poles. Because a circle is measured in degrees- 360° to be precise- a part of that circle is also measured in degrees. A north or south latitude can be no more than 90°, or that quarter of a circle lying between the North or South Pole and the equator.

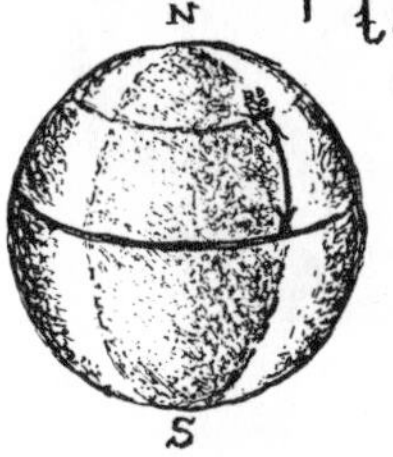

Each degree is equal to 60 nautical miles. Each degree can be further divided into 60 minutes, and each minute would therefore equal one nautical mile (thanks to the efforts of the French in 1756, the nautical mile was found equal to 6080 feet).

POSITION BY OBSERVATION~ Nature has supplied the navigator with celestial sign posts. If, for example, he could find the altitude of the sun at noon, he could compare this finding to a known position- a recorded number of degrees of the sun's angle with the horizon for the same day, month and year. A noon fix made it a deal easier, for the sun would then be directly in line with the meridian (the arc that was the distance from ship to equator=ab).

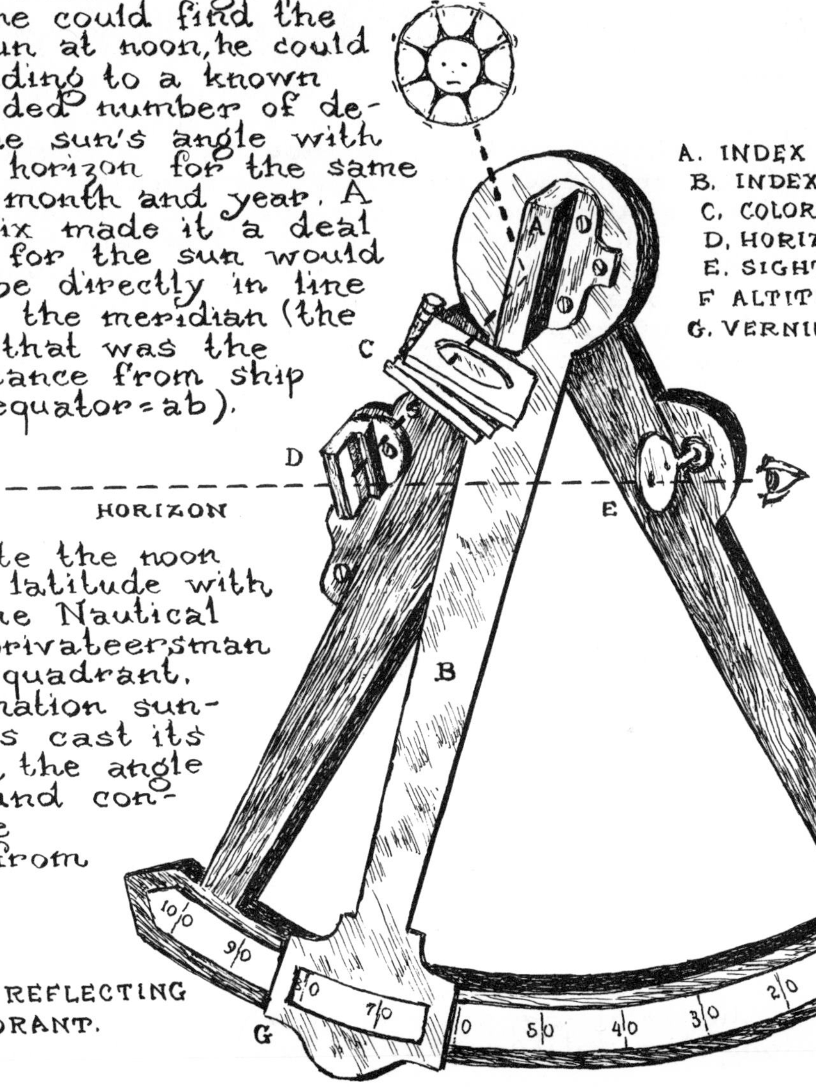

EQUATOR

A. INDEX GLASS.
B. INDEX.
C. COLORED GLASSES.
D. HORIZON GLASS.
E. SIGHT VANE.
F ALTITUDE SCALE.
G. VERNIER.

HORIZON

To translate the noon sun's angle into latitude with the tables in the Nautical Almanack, the privateersman reached for his quadrant. When his combination sundial and compass cast its shadow on noon, the angle was recorded and converted into the ship's distance from the equator.

HADLEY'S REFLECTING QUADRANT.

USING THE QUADRANT ~

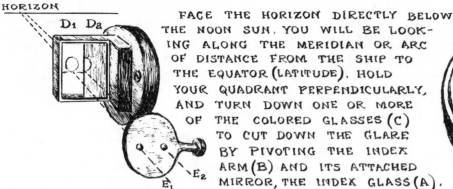

FACE THE HORIZON DIRECTLY BELOW THE NOON SUN. YOU WILL BE LOOK- ING ALONG THE MERIDIAN OR ARC OF DISTANCE FROM THE SHIP TO THE EQUATOR (LATITUDE). HOLD YOUR QUADRANT PERPENDICULARLY, AND TURN DOWN ONE OR MORE OF THE COLORED GLASSES (C) TO CUT DOWN THE GLARE BY PIVOTING THE INDEX ARM (B) AND ITS ATTACHED MIRROR, THE INDEX GLASS (A).

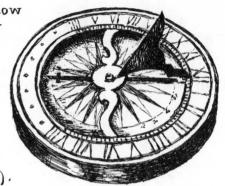

POCKET COMPASS AND SUN DIAL.

THE SUN'S IMAGE IS BROUGHT DOWN TO REFLECT IN THE CLEAR OUTER HALF OF THE HORIZON GLASS (D₁). THE IMAGE IS MOVED DOWN TO REST ON THE HORIZON- AS SEEN THROUGH THIS TRANSPARENT PART OF THE GLASS. VIEW THROUGH THE OUTER HOLE IN THE SIGHT VANE (E₁). IF, HOWEVER, THE SUN IS DIMMED BY CLOUDS OR HAZE, THE SILVERED INNER HALF OF THE HORIZON GLASS (D₂) IS USED. THE REFLECTED SUN IS THEN BISECTED BY THE LINE JOINING THE SILVERED AND TRANSPARENT GLASS. ITS LOWER EDGE ALSO RESTS ON THE HORIZON, AS SEEN THROUGH THE OUTER CLEAR GLASS THE POSITION OF THE INDEX VERNIER (G) ON THE SCALE (F) INDICATES THE ALTITUDE OF THE SUN.

LONGITUDE ~ is the distance east or west from a fixed point of reference~ England's Greenwich. The various longitudes are great circles passing through the North and South Poles dividing the equator and its parallel latitudes into twenty-four equal parts. Each division contains 15 degrees, the total circumference being 360 degrees. A point opposite to Greenwich on the globe would be recorded as either 180 degrees to the east or 180 degrees to the west. At the equator, each degree of longitude would be either sixty miles east or west, while at the North and South Pole the distance would diminish to zero.

To find the ship's longitude, one must carry a timepiece set to Greenwich time. Knowing this, and knowing the time on board, the difference in hours would be known. This difference could then be converted into degrees. The earth revolves on its axis every twenty-four hours~ therefore each hour equals 15 degrees, or 4 minutes equal to one degree. The navigator would then know the degrees of longitude east or west of Greenwich.

The problem~ and a very large problem it was ~ was having accurate Greenwich time aboard. The ordinary spring watches were much too sensitive to temperature changes and fell far short of the precision needed. The chronometer was the answer, but was too new and too scarce for use in the Revolutionary War. The six in existence were controlled by balances and springs to compensate for temperature changes, but it was later generations of seafarers who would benefit from this remarkable timekeeper.

Therefore, the privateer captain, along with his seagoing friends and enemies, did the best he could with the longitude problem. He would set his course well to one side of his destination when he reached the latitude of that port, he would sail due east or west along the latitude until he had a landfall.

POSITION BY DEDUCTION~

Rain, clouds or fog ~ one or all could plague the navigator trying to take a noon reading of the sun. To arrive at his position at sea, his latitude and longitude must be approximated by dead reckoning. When the century was younger, this process was known as "deduced position" or "deduced reckoning". By the Revolution, it was abbreviated to "ded reckoning" in the narrow columns of the log board and log book.

The navigator began with the known latitude and longitude of his port of departure. By chalking the proper information on his slate or log board, he could reckon his position at the end of the sea day ~ the following noon. At this time the information was permanently recorded in the log book, which was ruled and divided in the same manner as the slate.

H = **Hours** ~ from noon to noon.

K = **Knots per hour**. The speed of the vessel was recorded in knots, or the number of sea miles per hour. It was found by "heaving the log" every hour or two.

If a vessel made one nautical mile (6080 feet) an hour, a half-minute glass would measure the time taken to go $\frac{1}{120}$ th of that distance. Therefore she would sail 6080 ÷ 120, or 50 feet 8 inches after the half minute glass was turned.

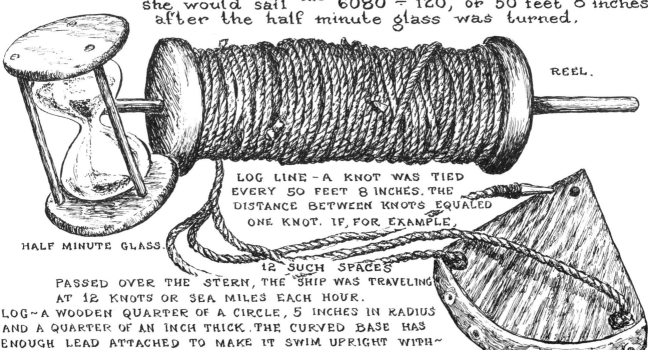

REEL.

LOG LINE ~ A KNOT WAS TIED EVERY 50 FEET 8 INCHES. THE DISTANCE BETWEEN KNOTS EQUALED ONE KNOT. IF, FOR EXAMPLE,

HALF MINUTE GLASS.

12 SUCH SPACES PASSED OVER THE STERN, THE SHIP WAS TRAVELING AT 12 KNOTS OR SEA MILES EACH HOUR.

LOG ~ A WOODEN QUARTER OF A CIRCLE, 5 INCHES IN RADIUS AND A QUARTER OF AN INCH THICK. THE CURVED BASE HAS ENOUGH LEAD ATTACHED TO MAKE IT SWIM UPRIGHT WITH~ OUT SINKING. ONE OF THE THREE SHORT LINES WAS CONNECTED

TO A WOODEN PEG. THIS WAS DISLODGED WHEN THE HEADING WAS FINISHED, ALLOWING THE LOG TO SKATE HOME WHEN THE LOG LINE WAS RETRIEVED.

"Heaving the log" instructions:
A seaman holds the reel, while another the half minute glass. The officer of the watch heaves the log over the ship's stern on the lee side. An un-marked distance is run off to carry the log out of the eddy of the ship's wake. When the first knot (often marked with a red rag) appears, he cries "turn!" The glass-holder answers "done!" and capsizes the glass. The moment the sand has run out, he cries "stop!" The reel is stopped, and the number of knots run off gives the miles per hour.

F = Fathoms ~ Sounding for the depth of the water gave further information on one's position. Measured in fathoms, it could be roughly estimated by extending both arms. More precisely, a fathom equaled six feet. The line was marked in fathoms by strips of leather and colored cloth.

LINE WAS ROVE THROUGH A LEATHER STRAP.

DEEP-SEA-LEAD ("DIPSEY") WOULD WEIGH 25 POUNDS AND UPWARDS. ITS LINE EXTENDED OVER 20 FATHOMS.

HAND-LEAD WEIGHED 6 TO 9 POUNDS AND HAD A LINE OF ABOUT 20 FATHOMS.

"Heaving the lead". Secure the free end of the line at the weather main chains. Swing like a pendulum three or four times, then swing it around your head for greater dis-tance and speed. The lead must be thrown far enough forward so that the line would be straight down by the time the lead reached the bottom.

TO INDICATE THE NATURE OF THE BOTTOM, THE HOLLOW AT THE BASE OF THE LEAD WAS FILLED WITH TALLOW. THIS PICKED UP SAND, SHELLS, GRAVEL AND PEBBLES.

Hand~lead~line markings. The line is marked at 2, 3, 5, 7, 10, 13, 15, 17 and 20 fathoms. The numbers between are called "deeps". For example:

"By the mark five!" = the five fathom mark is at the water's edge.

"By the dip four!" = an estimation of depth between marks.

"And a quarter five!"}
"And a half four!"} = if he judges the depth to be a quarter or a half more than any particular number.

"And a quarter less five!" = if the depth is three quarters more than a particular number, he calls it a quarter less than the next~as here at four fathoms and three quarters.

Deep~sea~lead. To use, the ship's headway must not exceed three or four knots. If not, the ship must reduce its headway to take the sounding. Depths of over 30 or 40 fathoms are difficult to take.

SLIDING COVER.

COURSE ~ as steered by the compass.

GLASS COVER.

UNDER SIDE OF COMPASS CARD WITH TWO BENT STEEL MAGNETIZED WIRES.

COMPASS CARD.

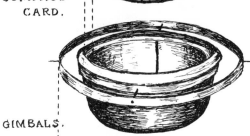

CUT-AWAY OF WOODEN COMPASS BOWL.

GIMBALS.

THE MAGNETIZED COMPASS CARD REVOLVED FREELY TO POINT TO MAGNETIC NORTH. THE LUBBER LINE, POSITIONED IN LINE WITH THE SHIP'S KEEL, WAS ALWAYS ON THE COURSE. THE COMPASS COURSE READING WAS THAT COMPASS POINT THAT WAS NEAREST THE LINE.

THE TWO BRASS GIMBAL RINGS KEPT THE COMPASS LEVEL.

THE DOG VANE WAS MADE OF CORK DISCS HOLDING CHICKEN FEATHERS. WHEN TIED IN THE RIGGING, IT WOULD DETECT THE MOST FEEBLE BREEZE. ON WINDLESS DAYS, SEA WATER WAS USED TO SOAK DOWN SAILS ~ THE BETTER TO CATCH THE BREEZE. DRY CANVAS WOULD LET AIR ESCAPE.

"BITTACLE" (NOW KNOWN AS BINNACLE) ~ A CUPBOARD~LIKE BOX HOUSING THE COMPASS, AS WELL AS THE LOG BOARD, LAMP AND OTHER NAVIGATIONAL GEAR.

Wind ~ A privateer, heading for England to plague her shipping, would make the west to east voyage in four or five weeks. But when returning ~ working east to west against the prevailing winds ~ it would take five, six or more weeks. Keeping a practiced nose to the wind would make the most of one's moving power.

The elasticity of air gives it an expanding or spreading motion. When under such influences as the heat of the sun, the air rushes in to restore the equilibrium. Wind is the result ~ and there are several kinds that the mariner knew well.

The trade winds blow constantly from the same region. For example, these predictable winds blow from the east in the Atlantic and Pacific oceans between the latitudes of 30°N and 30° S. And there are the monsoons, blowing half the year one way and opposite the other half. And lastly, there are the variable winds ~ those fickle and often dangerous winds that appear from any direction and any place.

Leeway ~ The sideward drift of the ship to the leeward ~ away from the direction of the wind. The officer of the watch commonly corrected the course for leeway before chalking it on the log ~ board.

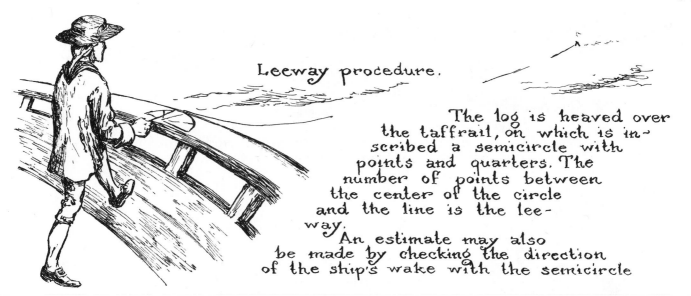

Leeway procedure.

The log is heaved over the taffrail, on which is inscribed a semicircle with points and quarters. The number of points between the center of the circle and the line is the leeway.

An estimate may also be made by checking the direction of the ship's wake with the semicircle

CHARTS

Hours, Knots, Fathoms, Course, Winds, Leeway, and Work - all gave the captain a rough idea where he could locate his privateer on a chart. (Maps, not charts, are of land for landlubbers.) Gerhardus Mercator, a chart-maker of the sixteenth century managed to turn the round earth into a flat piece of paper.

BRITISH BRASS COURSE PROTRACTOR, DRAWN $\frac{4}{5}$ths SIZE.

AMERICAN DIVIDERS - REVOLUTIONARY. DRAWN $\frac{4}{5}$ths SIZE.

He did so by drawing the latitude and longitude as straight lines perpendicular to one another. Obviously, the plotting and measuring on a chart made drawing one's course a deal easier. True - the farther away from the equator the chart was drawn, the more distorted it became. But it worked well enough for seamen to use Mercator's charts hundreds of years later.

Charts, navigational almanacs, dividers, protractors and quadrants were the personal property of the captain. Such equipment varied according to availability and the captain's means. Whatever he lacked, a decent telescope was a must for keeping a sharp lookout ahead.

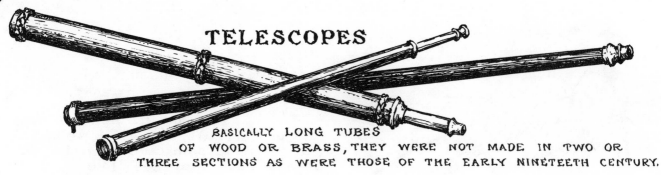

TELESCOPES

BASICALLY LONG TUBES
OF WOOD OR BRASS, THEY WERE NOT MADE IN TWO OR
THREE SECTIONS AS WERE THOSE OF THE EARLY NINETEETH CENTURY.

TO CHASE

Some sharp-eyed sailor would have a hundred pounds in his pocket for spotting the sail ahead ~ if it proved to be a prize. There were several time-honored steps that the privateer captain mulled in his mind before he took to the chase.

I. Are we faster? Get on the same tack and course as the stranger. Hoist the same sail. Now set her position in your compass. If your sharp-hulled craft is the faster, the stranger's sails will soon draw a point aft. If both are equal sailors, she will keep the same compass point. But if she draws points forward, a chase is pointless.

II. To chase to the windward. Having the faster vessel, you must set your course the same as the stranger.

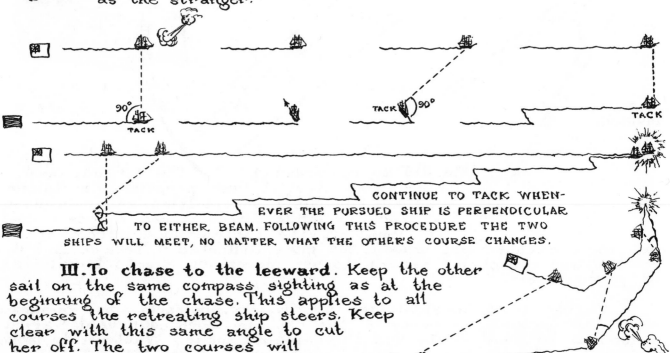

CONTINUE TO TACK WHEN-
EVER THE PURSUED SHIP IS PERPENDICULAR
TO EITHER BEAM. FOLLOWING THIS PROCEDURE THE TWO
SHIPS WILL MEET, NO MATTER WHAT THE OTHER'S COURSE CHANGES.

III. To chase to the leeward. Keep the other sail on the same compass sighting as at the beginning of the chase. This applies to all courses the retreating ship steers. Keep clear with this same angle to cut her off. The two courses will sooner or later intersect.

IV Scudding ~ When sailing before a heavy gale, carry enough lofty sail to keep her freely and fairly before the sea. There is a real danger that the waves will travel faster than the ship, and might overtake and break over her. Further, the height of the waves might run so high that any lower forward sails might be becalmed. Therefore a close-reefed main topsail should be set to catch the wind well above the waves. By increasing headway, the waves will strike abaft with less force. The heavily ladened merchant ship is more liable to get "pooped" (the waves breaking over the poop or stern deck) during the chase.

V. A failing wind ~ Even though every last knife aboard be stuck in the mainmast, there are times when such powerful persuasion cannot muster a breeze. Oar power must be broken out and used to close with the enemy.

Captain Jonathan Haraden, commanding the privateer "General Pickering" (sixteen six pounders and thirty men ~ the prize crews having left) was making little headway under a failing breeze. At the entrance to Bilboa harbor, a Spanish port on the Bay of Biscay, she met with a rugged enemy, the British privateer "Archilles" (forty guns and one hundred and fifty men). One witness said the American looked like a long boat alongside a ship! The "Archilles" did her best to grapple, but the "General Pickering" manned her sweeps and pulled away. Not only that, but she maneuvered again and again under the enemy's stern and raked her fore and aft. For three hours she tore away at "Archilles'" heel until the crippled enemy limped out of range.

SWEEPS WERE RUN THROUGH THE OAR PORTS THAT WERE INTERSPERSED BETWEEN THE GUN PORTS ALONG THE BULWARKS.

WOODEN THOLE PIN, DRAWN $\frac{1}{2}$ SIZE.

VI. Closing to windward ~ The attacking ship, necessarily being the better sailer, has the advantage of maneuverability on the weather gauge. The leeward vessel, on the other hand, is sluggish tacking to the windward. She might also be hulled by cannon fire below her water line while heeled over by the wind.

While moving to the windward quarter, cross the enemy's stern and luff your canvas with the helm alee. Rake her stern with your biggest guns as they pass. Aim well for the rudder, tiller, and their block and tackle. A disabled vessel will fall easy prey. Also a few cannon balls, smashing everything in their path fore and aft, does much to dishearten the other vessel.

BLUFF

Lives and powder could be spared and the prize won by a sharp bit of Yankee psychology. A few naval uniforms, obvious among the bare-chested, cutlass-waving crew could do much to make a faint-hearted merchantman strike her colors.

From Gloucester, Massachusetts, hailed a famous privateersman with a bottomless bag of tricks. Jonathan Haraden covered his gun ports with painted canvas to look the part of a vulnerable American merchantmen. When a Britisher bore in for the bait, she would be met with a crushing broadside. It should be noted that this remarkable seaman never lost a ship, and his captured war booty was of inestimable value to Washington's efforts ashore.

CAPTAIN HARADEN

In 1780, when Captain Haraden was on a night cruise off the Bay of Biscay, his privateer "General Pickering" suddenly came upon the British armed brig "Golden Eagle". The American's voice came through the darkness loud and clear- either his enemy strike instantly or he would sink her, for he was "a United States frigate of the heaviest class". The English captain, after his surrender, was more than distressed to find that his late command was actually of equal strength to the "General Pickering".

BATTLE STATIONS!

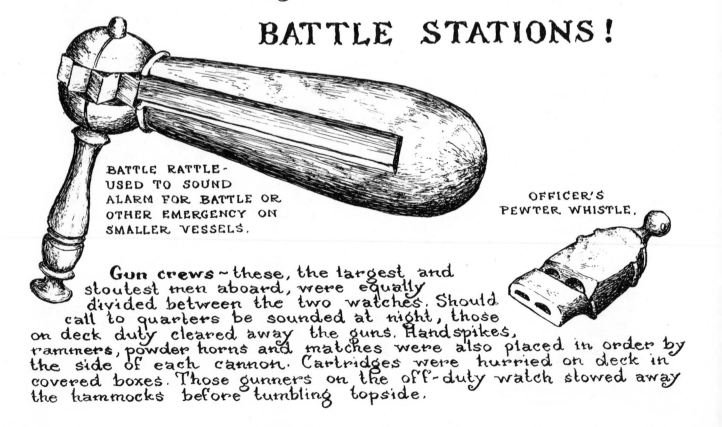

BATTLE RATTLE-USED TO SOUND ALARM FOR BATTLE OR OTHER EMERGENCY ON SMALLER VESSELS.

OFFICER'S PEWTER WHISTLE.

Gun crews ~ these, the largest and stoutest men aboard, were equally divided between the two watches. Should call to quarters be sounded at night, those on deck duty cleared away the guns. Handspikes, rammers, powder horns and matches were also placed in order by the side of each cannon. Cartridges were hurried on deck in covered boxes. Those gunners on the off-duty watch stowed away the hammocks before tumbling topside.

With both gun watches on deck for action, one carried cutlasses and would be the first boarders. The other watch carried pikes and made up the second wave of boarders - or repel boarders with a change of fortune. The gun captains, chosen for their steadiness, sharp vision and quick thought, supervised and checked the handling of the big guns.

Topmen - here were the young and active seamen with a sprinkling of ordinary seamen, landsmen and boys. Under the watchful eye of the boatswain, they went aloft to trim sails, ready extra rigging for repairs, and secured sail yards that other- wise might crash down with a cannon shot.

Marines - the "gentlemen volunteers" scrambled for the mast trees and deck positions with their small arms.

Firemen, quarter-gunners and **powder boys** - stationed below to protect the ports and make ready to extinguish any fires.

Carpenter - made ready with shot plugs and all gear necessary to repair hull and pumps.

Cook - to galley to extinguish all fires!

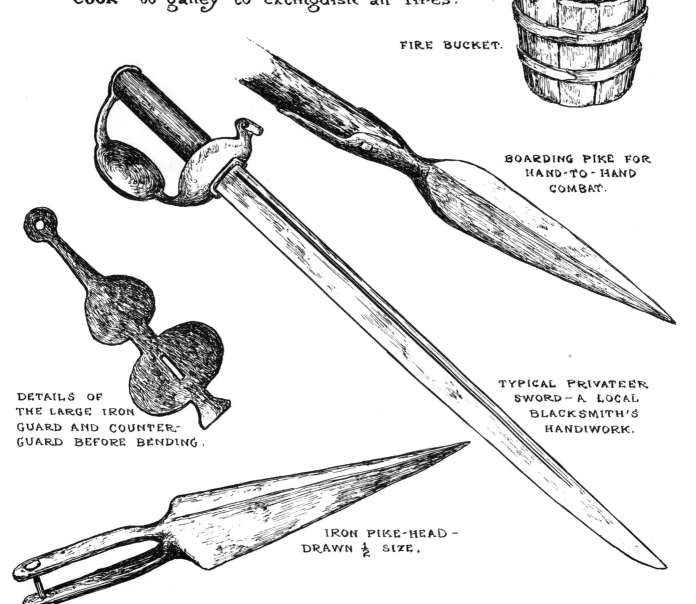

FIRE BUCKET.

BOARDING PIKE FOR HAND-TO-HAND COMBAT.

DETAILS OF THE LARGE IRON GUARD AND COUNTER- GUARD BEFORE BENDING.

TYPICAL PRIVATEER SWORD - A LOCAL BLACKSMITH'S HANDIWORK.

IRON PIKE-HEAD - DRAWN ½ SIZE.

ACTION IN THE MAIN~TOP

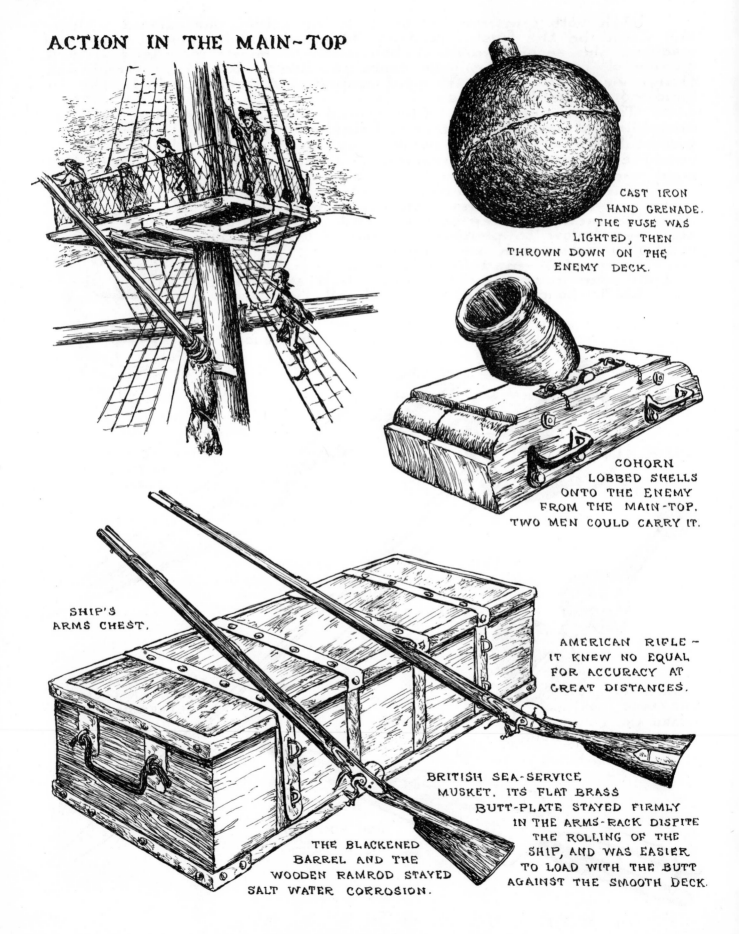

CAST IRON HAND GRENADE. THE FUSE WAS LIGHTED, THEN THROWN DOWN ON THE ENEMY DECK.

COHORN LOBBED SHELLS ONTO THE ENEMY FROM THE MAIN-TOP. TWO MEN COULD CARRY IT.

SHIP'S ARMS CHEST.

AMERICAN RIFLE — IT KNEW NO EQUAL FOR ACCURACY AT GREAT DISTANCES.

THE BLACKENED BARREL AND THE WOODEN RAMROD STAYED SALT WATER CORROSION.

BRITISH SEA-SERVICE MUSKET. ITS FLAT BRASS BUTT-PLATE STAYED FIRMLY IN THE ARMS-RACK DISPITE THE ROLLING OF THE SHIP, AND WAS EASIER TO LOAD WITH THE BUTT AGAINST THE SMOOTH DECK.

The fighting tops~ those platforms at the junction of the main and topmasts~ became tiny fortresses. There were enough hand grenades, stink pots, swivel guns and an occasional cohorn to rain destruction on an exposed deck. The marksmen saw to their muskets. Smooth-bored and quickly loaded, they could hope for some degree of accuracy~ provided the enemy was less than eighty yards away.

Those fortunate to own rifles~ spirally~grooved bores that snugged about a patched ball~ could expect an accuracy of three times that of the musket. Captain Joshua Barney was a man who appreciated a methodical picking off of officers and gun captains. Before casting off from Philadelphia with his privateer "Hyder Ally", he saw to it that his complement included a number of Bucks County marksmen.

STINK POT

A DEVILISH CONCOCT- ION OF SALTPETER (SODIUM NITRATE), BRIM- STONE (SULFUR), ASAFETIDA (MALODOROUS GUM RESIN OF ORIENTAL PLANTS OF THE CARROT FAMILY), AND DECAYED FISH WAS PACKED INTO EARTHEN JUGS WHEN THE WICK(CALLED OX-TAIL) WAS LIT, THE FOUL AND SUFFO- CATING MIXTURE WAS HURLED DOWN FROM THE MAIN-TREE, THE NAUSEATING SMOKE THAT SPREAD THROUGH THE HOLD AND ON DECK COULD GIVE AN OB- STINATE ENEMY SECOND THOUGHTS ON RESISTANCE.

BOARDING

THE PRIVATEERS' SPECIALTY

CALCULATED COLLISIONS ~The "Hyder Ally" (sixteen six pounders and a crew of one hundred and twenty) was running down the Delaware River early in April, 1782 as the escort ship for a flock of merchantmen, when she met an old friend and a new enemy. The latter was the privateer "General Washington" (twenty six pounders), captured by a British squadron and pressed into service because of her sharp, swift lines. Renamed the "General Monk", she moved up quickly to overtake and board the American vessel.

Captain Barney had different thoughts. Being somewhat ahead of his enemy, he swerved abruptly to starboard~ directly in the other's path. The "General Monk"'s bowsprit and jib gear became hopelessly tangled in the "Hyder Ally"'s fore-mast. The British were unable to board over the length of their bowsprit and through the boarding nets that Barney had prudently erected. His starboard guns churned up the length of the enemy's deck, while the Bucks County sharp-shooters picked off any who attempted to play swivel guns on their tormentors. In half an hour the "General Monk" was again the "General Washington".

A collision at sea is a ready-made boarding opportunity~ or a disaster for the attacking ship. If you can foul the enemy's bowsprit in your main-shrouds, you can rake his length at your pleasure~ as did Captain Barney. As a rule of thumb, get a bit to the leeward. When you are one or two ship lengths ahead (depending on your speed), shiver your sails~that is, spill

the wind by luffing your canvas or laying them flat against the mast. Put your helm hard a-lee and you have his bow locked in your rigging. She's yours for the taking.

But there are few fools at sea, and the British have the least of these. Therefore you had best have a few alternatives in your bag of tricks.

WIND

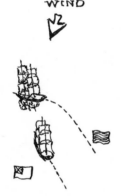

If you overshoot, you can at least rake her bow.

If you undershoot across her course, your bowsprit might find itself trapped in the others rigging.

Range close to your enemy. If she suspects your intentions, she might put the helm hard a-lee as soon as your vessel veers across her path.

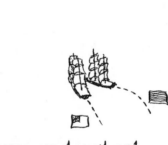

GRAPPLING ~ The
calculated collision securely binds the two vessels together for boarding. The more usual method, however, is to approach the enemy near enough to throw your grapplings on board. The ropes of these multi-clawed irons are secured to the lower yard-arms, at the forecastle, gangways and the like.

A unique grappling iron was used by that equally unique privateer John Manly. The captain was cruising off New York harbor on July 25, 1779. Several sail on the weather bow brought the crew scrambling. When his sharp-sailing privateer "Jason" (twenty guns and one hundred men) was within two cannon shot, Manly gave the call to quarters. Then came an unusual second order, and the best bower anchor was broken out! Running alongside the enemy, the American privateersman's anchor ripped into and held firmly the enemy's fore rigging. The "Jason" fired every gun that bore. The stunned British yielded to the boarders, the tangled rigging was cut away, and Manly spread his canvas to take after the other sail.

HOW TO BOARD~

To chase and board, a captain intuitively kept his keel at an efficient angle to the wind. He might put it this way. A vessel cannot sail into the eye of the wind. Fore-and-aft rigs can point into the wind no more than 40° when close hauled. Square riggers can point no better than 55°. However, a wise seaman never sails as close to the wind as possible. This "pinching" will give the lowest speed, and the lower the speed, the greater the side drift. Therefore you must point as high as possible while keeping good speed.

"Running" with the wind astern is best done with the wind within 30° of either side, for the aft sails steal the wind from those foreward.

WIND

40°

55°

"PINCHING"

"RUNNING"

30°

WIND

BOARD TO WINDWARD

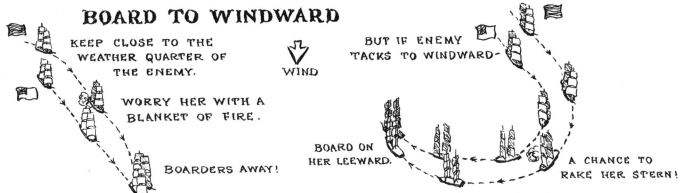

KEEP CLOSE TO THE WEATHER QUARTER OF THE ENEMY.

WIND

WORRY HER WITH A BLANKET OF FIRE.

BOARDERS AWAY!

BUT IF ENEMY TACKS TO WINDWARD-

BOARD ON HER LEEWARD.

A CHANCE TO RAKE HER STERN!

LUFF SAILS WHEN GOING WINDWARD TO KEEP ASTERN.

IF SHE TACKS TO WINDWARD -

YOUR SPEED, BEING BETTER ON THE WEATHER SIDE, PERMITS YOU TO MAKE A TIGHT ARC. YOU SHORTLY WILL BE ON HER STERN.

IF YOU COME ABOUT TOO FAST TO THE WIND, SHORTEN YOUR SAIL AND RAKE HER AS YOU PASS.

BOARD TO LEEWARD

WIND

WHEN YOUR FORECASTLE IS ABREAST OF THE ENEMY'S MAINMAST, LUFF YOUR SAILS AND PUT HELM HARD A-LEE TO CLOSE IN.
PASS HER LEE QUARTER SO CLOSE THAT YOUR CAT-HEAD ALMOST TOUCHES AND SHE CANNOT RAKE YOU WITH HER GUNS.
FOLLOW IN WAKE WITHIN A PISTOL SHOT.

BUT IF SHE TACKS TO LEE-WARD, YOU ARE IN DANGER!
KEEP A SHARP EYE THAT THE ENEMY DOESN'T SUDDENLY MAKE STERNWAY BY SPILLING HER WIND AND TURN-ING HELM HARD A-LEE. YOUR BOWSPRIT MAY ENGAGE IN THE MAIN SHROUDS. SO TRAPPED, SHE CAN RAKE YOUR LENGTH AT WILL.

OR

VEER AWAY FROM HER WHEN YOU ARE ABREAST OF THE ENEMY — AS THOUGH YIELDING TO HER FIRE. HOPEFULLY, SHE WILL VEER TOWARD YOU TO PLAY MORE CANNON FIRE UPON YOU. PUT YOUR HELM HARD A-LEE AND QUICKLY TRIM SAILS. BE QUICK AND YOU WILL BE ABOARD IN A MOMENT.

BOARDING AN ENEMY AT ANCHOR-WITH THE WIND

WIND

YOUR HUNT WILL SOON HAVE THIS SITTING DUCK IN YOUR PRIZE BAG. APPROACH ON THE WEATHER SIDE, SPILL YOUR WIND AND DRIFT INTO HER. ANNOY HER WITH YOUR BROAD-SIDE AS YOU MOVE IN.

LET GO YOUR ANCHOR AT THE TIME YOU BOARD. IF THE ENEMY CUTS HER CABLES TO DRIVE ON SHORE, SHE WILL HAVE NO COMPANY.

BOARDING AN ENEMY AT ANCHOR~ AGAINST WIND

WIND

NO ATTEMPT SHOULD BE MADE TO TOW YOUR PRIVATEER INTO BOARDING POSITION. YOU AND YOUR LONG BOATS WILL BE TORN APART BY THE ENEMY'S GUNFIRE.

RATHER, APPROACH TO THE WINDWARD. STOP YOUR HEADWAY BY SPILLING THE WIND FROM YOUR MIZZEN-TOPSAIL AND FORE-TOPSAIL. WHEN YOU HAVE PASSED THE ENEMY ABOUT A SHIP'S LENGTH, LET GO YOUR ANCHOR AND DRIFT HEAD TO WIND. PAY OUT YOUR CABLE AND FALL OFF UNTIL THE WIND BRINGS YOU ALONGSIDE THE ENEMY. RAKE HER BEFORE YOU THROW THE GRAPPLES.

BRITISH NAVAL BOARDING
PISTOL WITH FOLDING BLADE.

PRIVATEER FLINTLOCK BLUNDERBUSS
(TOP JAW AND RAMROD MISSING), SWIVEL
YOKE PRESENT.

BOAT HOOK.

BRITISH BOARDING
AXE. HEAD AND
HAFT WERE PAINTED
BLACK.

BROAD ARROW
SHOWS BRITISH
OWNERSHIP.

THREE BOARDING ADVENTURES
(One thwarted by crowbars!)

Remember the two hour battle between the "General Pickering", Captain Jonathan Haraden commanding, and the
larger and more heavily armed
"Archilles"? Haraden was short on
ammunition and he ordered the gun
muzzles packed with crowbars! Observers
reported that this flight of huge arrows
"made hash" of the "Archilles" decks. She
had the good fortune to limp out of
the "General Pickering's" range, any thoughts
of boarding long forgotten. Haraden pursued
and offered his gunners sizable rewards if they
could carry away one of the enemy's mast.

On September 6, 1781, the privateer "Congress"
(twenty-four guns and crew of two hundred-Captain
George Geddes of Philadelphia) tangled with the
slower and smaller British ship "Savage" off the
Georgia coast. Little love was lost on this shal-
low draft Britisher, for she had sailed into
countless small bays and rivers, spotted likely
plantations to raid, then returned under cover
of darkness. But the "Congress" found she had
a wildcat by the tail! The two ships battled
to a draw in such close range that some men
were singed by the other's cannon fire. Some
crewmen even threw smaller sized cannon balls

at the enemy.

The battered "Congress" dressed her wounds and returned to the wallowing "Savage ~ mastless, rudderless, and her captain dead. None-the-less, the "Savage" lived up to her name, battling with courage and spirit that had made England the greatest sea power in the world. After half an hour of hard slugging, Captain Geddes ordered boarders away. The men had gathered in the waist, sleeves rolled up and bare feet dipped in sand for a surer hold. Pikes and cutlasses had been passed out. At that moment, the only surviving officer of the "Savage," the boatswain, waved his cap in surrender. (Colors could not be struck, for they had long since been shot away.) The casualty list was fairly equal ~ thirty-two Britishers and thirty Americans.

The British privateer "Three Brothers" had been plaguing Long Island Sound. On February 20th, 1783, this vessel was sighted near Stratford Point. According to plan, forty Continental soldiers under Captain Brewster hurried aboard the swift-sailing sloop "Julius Caesar" (Amos Hubbell, captain). The Americans fell in with the British privateer and received a broadside for their trouble ~ followed by swivels and musketry. The American troops remained hidden until the "Three Brothers" closed for boarding. Then they jumped up, discharged a single volley of musket balls, and boarded the British vessel with fixed bayonets. It was an unusual and success-ful piece of team-work between land and sea forces. The captain of the "Three Brothers" and several of his crewmen were snuffed out in the single volley.

INSTRUCTIONS FOR FIRE FIGHTING ~ After

securing your prisoners, get your ship before the wind if the fire is on deck and forward. If the fire is aft, haul close to the wind. Muster the men at their stations, and reduce sails to top-sails. If the courses, or mainrails are not hauled up smartly, they will strike a current of air down the hatchways ~ and also will be liable to catch fire. Call away the firemen and have all grates cover-ed with tarpaulins and the ports closed. The gunners and his mates will report immediately to the magazine, ready to douse the powder at a moment's notice. The carpenters will rig the pumps. The spar-deck division should clear away the boats, see to their equipment, and get them ready for hoisting out.

ON STOPPING LEAKS ~ A sinking ship is a poor way

to stop a fire. To plug a shot hole, double a sail canvas and haul it in position by ropes under the keel or out of the hawse-holes. The smaller the canvas, the less likely it will be torn away when the canvas becomes saturated, it be-comes tolerably watertight, much as a fireman's hose. The leak may not be completely stopped, but it will certainly reduce it until more permanent repairs can be made.

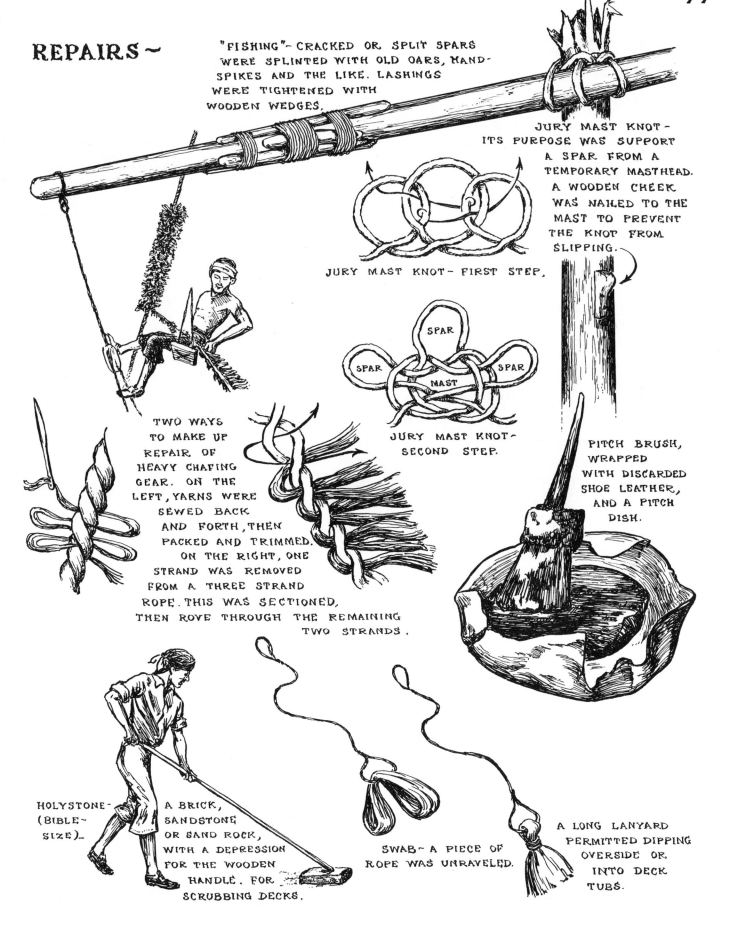

REPAIRS ~

"FISHING" ~ CRACKED OR SPLIT SPARS WERE SPLINTED WITH OLD OARS, HAND-SPIKES AND THE LIKE. LASHINGS WERE TIGHTENED WITH WOODEN WEDGES.

JURY MAST KNOT ~ ITS PURPOSE WAS SUPPORT A SPAR FROM A TEMPORARY MASTHEAD. A WOODEN CHEEK WAS NAILED TO THE MAST TO PREVENT THE KNOT FROM SLIPPING.

JURY MAST KNOT ~ FIRST STEP.

SPAR

SPAR

SPAR

MAST

JURY MAST KNOT ~ SECOND STEP.

PITCH BRUSH, WRAPPED WITH DISCARDED SHOE LEATHER, AND A PITCH DISH.

TWO WAYS TO MAKE UP REPAIR OF HEAVY CHAFING GEAR. ON THE LEFT, YARNS WERE SEWED BACK AND FORTH, THEN PACKED AND TRIMMED. ON THE RIGHT, ONE STRAND WAS REMOVED FROM A THREE STRAND ROPE. THIS WAS SECTIONED, THEN ROVE THROUGH THE REMAINING TWO STRANDS.

HOLYSTONE ~ (BIBLE~SIZE)~ A BRICK, SANDSTONE OR SAND ROCK, WITH A DEPRESSION FOR THE WOODEN HANDLE. FOR SCRUBBING DECKS.

SWAB ~ A PIECE OF ROPE WAS UNRAVELED.

A LONG LANYARD PERMITTED DIPPING OVERSIDE OR INTO DECK TUBS.

SEA SURGERY

CROOKED NEEDLE WITH LIGATURE OF WAXED SHOEMAKER'S THREAD TO COMPRESS THE ARTERY WITHOUT CUTTING.

READY FOR BATTLE~

When action is imminent and as soon as all hands are called to quarters, see to:

PLATFORM ~ Request the first lieutenant, with the captain's permission, to lay a platform of planks, close together, eight, ten or twelve feet square, on a tier of smooth, even casks.

~ Locate in one of the cable tiers if it is available; otherwise, set up your surgery in the afterhold. If your privateer be small and has no cockpit, find a spot as near the afterhold as possible.

PREPARATION ~ Lay out your equipment as follows:

1. On one side of the platform, lay out your capital instruments, needles and ligatures, lint, styptics, bandages, splints, compresses, pledges spread with yellow basilicon or some other proper digestive, thread, tape, tow, pins, and new and old linen cloth.

2. Prepare the medicine chest with ung. basil. ~ c, gum. elem. ~ sambucin; ol. lin. ~; oli-var. c. ~terebinth; bals. terebinth; tinct. styp - thaebaic; sp. c.c. per se. ~ vol. aromat. ~ lavend. c. There should be wine, punch or grog, and vinigar in plenty.

3. A bucket of water to put sponges in; another to receive blood from operations.

4. Dry swabs to keep the platform dry.

5. A water cask full of water, head knocked in, to be dipped out as needed.

6. Seamans' bedding laid side by side.

~ Instruct mates and assistants as to their stations.

~ Have the first officer quarter a number of hands in the cockpit, should assistance be needed in battle.

~ Send any crew, too sick to go to quarters, into the hold-or some such area out of the way~ with their hammocks and bedding. The platform is only for wounded. Have a man check on the sick occasionally. In case of faintness, give them a little cordial.

~ Light a number of large candles as soon as engagement begins.

SCREW TOURNIQUET THE STRONG WORSTED TAPE TIGHTENS ABOUT THE EXTREMITY AS THE SCREW TURNS TO COMPRESS THE ARTERY.

SCALPEL.

RETRACTOR SEPARATES LIPS OF THE WOUND.

TENACULUM PIERCES AND DRAWS OUT AN ARTERY FOR TYING.

AMERICAN AMPUTATION SAW.

CAPITAL INSTRUMENTS.

DURING THE ACTION~

As the wounded come down, take care of those in the most immediate danger; otherwise, dress the wounds as they come.

~Have a mate apply a tourniquet to a limb off or any violent hemorrhage, if you are in the middle of a capital operation. The tourniquet should remain in place, ready to stop a fresh hemorrhage. Instruct patient to tighten it, should he feel the wound bleeding before help comes.

~When readying a patient for a capital operation, encourage him, promise to treat him tenderly, that you will finish as soon as possible, and that you will not cut more than is necessary. At the same time, act as though you are unaffected by their groans and complaints, but in no case, behave rashly or cruelly.

~Insist that the wounded, once dressed and little hurt, return to their stations at quarters. If they lag, threaten to report them after the engagement is over. There are some dastardly fellows who have even been known to stand in the way of a recoiling gun carriage in order to go to the doctor. There is no place for cowards, including your surgical platform.

AFTER THE ENGAGEMENT~ Give a proper diet and medicines suitable to the symptomatic fever and such.

~After seeing to your wounded, acquaint the captain of the number of injured, the nature of wounds, and if any are likely to prove mortal. Ask him to order cradles to hold the wounded men and their bedding. The cradles to hold the wounded men and their bedding. The cradles should be in a berth by themselves, and each should be well cleated and secured to the deck and sides of the ship. They should be so placed that you can easily go between them and tend to the dressings.

MEDICINE CHEST USED BY DR. JOSHUA FISHER IN THE REVOLUTIONARY WAR.

COOK BOOK MEDICINE

Privateering vessels were many. Physicians and surgeons were few. Frequently the art of healing fell on the shoulders of the captain of the smaller vessels—or one of his officers. Reading ability, not diagnostic skill, was the prerequisite. A sick seaman would first list his complaints. The medical text was then thumbed through until these symptoms matched the description.

Once the disease was established, one need only follow the appropriate treatment.

Further down the page, medications to be given were listed by number. No need to contend with jaw-breaking Latin labels~only match the numbered vials and bottles in the medicine chest and give the prescribed amount. Hopefully, this and a dose of salt air would bring on recovery.

PRISONERS

Dr Solomon Drowne served his hitch as a Continental Army surgeon throughout the war - or rather, all but seventeen days. This was the time he caught the privateering fever and signed aboard the privateering sloop "Hope" (seven guns and twenty crew). Sailing from Providence, Rhode Island, his home town, he recorded his adventures of his 1780 cruise with all the precision of a surgeon. Here are a few excerpts concerning the capture of prisoners.

"October 15th. ...There seems something awful in the preparation for an attack and the immediate prospect of an action. She hauls up her courses and hoists English colors. I take my station in the cabin, where [I] remain not long before I hear the huzza on deck in consequence of her striking. Send our boat for the captain and his papers. She sailed from Kingston, Jamaica, upward of forty days since, in a fleet, and was bound to New York, Captain William Small, commander. She has ten men on board and four excellent 4-pounders. Her cargo consists of one hundred and forty-nine puncheons, twenty-three hogsheads, three quarter casks and nine barrels of rum, and twenty hogsheads of muscovado sugar. [We] send two prize masters and ten men on board, get the prisoners on board our vessel and take the prize in tow. Stand towards Egg Harbor. ......"

"October 19th ..... Have our pistols hung up in the cabin, to be in readiness for the prisoners should they take it in their heads to rise upon the watch in the night."

This was a wise precaution, and if there were the least danger of an uprising, the prisoners were clapped in irons. Veteran privateersmen had an old saying - "One to every gun." It was a fortunate vessel who took the same number of prizes on a single cruise as there were cannon aboard. The privateer "Hope", by this rule of thumb, was well within their limit of seven. Taking more than this courted disaster, for the absence of prize crews and increasing numbers of prisoners in the hold made an uprising a real threat.

LEG IRON.

A case in point appeared in the Boston Gazette of December 9th, 1776, where a letter by an Englishman was quoted concerning the capture of the American privateer sloop Yankee (nine guns and sixty men, Henry Johnson commanding). "..... THE CAPTURE OF THE PRIVATEER WAS SOLEY OWING TO THE ILL-JUDGED LENITY AND BROTHERLY KINDNESS OF CAPTAIN JOHNSON WHO, NOT CONSIDERING HIS ENGLISH PRISONERS IN THE SAME LIGHT THAT HE WOULD FRENCHMEN OR SPANIARDS, PUT THEM UNDER NO SORT OF CONFINEMENT, BUT PERMITTED THEM TO WALK THE DECKS AS FREELY AS HIS OWN PEOPLE, AT ALL TIMES. TAKING ADVANTAGE OF THIS INDULGENCE THE PRISONERS ONE

DAY, WATCHING THEIR OPPORTUNITY WHEN MOST OF THE PRIVATEER'S PEOPLE WERE BELOW AND ASLEEP, SHUT DOWN THE HATCHES AND TOOK THE VESSEL WITHOUT FORCE."

HANDCUFFS.

BROKEN →

There was no such consideration for American prisoners. Any such freedom-seeking rebel was officially declared a pirate and a traitor to His Majesty. Such high treason on the high seas or in the American colonies was punishable by death. Fortunately, not a single Yankee privateersman's life was sacrificed to the gallows. An act of Parliament sidestepped the issue by declaring that such traitors would not go on trial until January 1st, 1778. This date was extended as the war progressed. If it went badly, it would be prudent to treat such as prisoners of war rather than treasonous subjects of King George III. And if the war went well, the trials would proceed without repercussions.

The treatment of American captives was just shy of hanging. Nathaniel Fanning, in his "Narrative", gave a fairly characteristic picture of the heavy-handed British. Fanning had sailed as a prize-master from Boston on May 26, 1778 on the newly constructed privateer brig "Angelica" (sixteen guns, ninety-eight men and boys, William Dennis commanding). Captured and placed on board the British frigate "Andromeda", they were first paraded on the quarter deck in the presence of "····their great and mighty general ····· the celebrated General Howe, of Bunker Hill memory, ·····. The general asked us a number of insignificant questions, among which was, 'If we were willing to engage in his majesty's service?' We having answered pretty unanimously in the negative, he then upbraided us with these words, 'You are a set of rebels, and it is more than probable that you will all be hanged on our arrival at Portsmouth.'"

Following this welcome aboard, the master at arms and some crewmen made a pretext of searching the privateers' baggage for concealed knives. The baggage was never seen again. On the way to the ship's hold, some of the "Jack Tars" ordered the prisoners to halt and began to strip them of their clothes, saying, "Come come! shipmates, these fine things will only be a plague to you, as the climate is very hot where you are bound, (meaning the ship's hold;)·····." They were given frocks and trousers and sent into

BRITISH GENL. WM. HOWE.

the hold. There they received no food for twenty hours - thereafter but two thirds the usual prisoner of war allowance. The captain and General Howe "...were deaf to our complaints and answered that we were treated with too much lenity, being considered as rebels, whose crimes were of such an aggravated kind that we should be shewn no mercy."

Mercy was not entirely wanting, however. Once every twenty-four hours, the prisoners were allowed on deck, one at a time. Then back to the oven in the pit of the ship - hot enough for most of the men to go stark naked. There, the closely packed privateers-men stewed in their own juices until the boiling point was reached. The enterprising and liberty-loving Yankees laid plans to take over the ship - one of His Majesty's mighty men-of-war! but word reached enemy ears before the plot could be hatched. The food was just enough to keep a man alive - and half a pint of water per man each day.

The prisoners remedied their hunger pangs by prying a plank from a partition that led to the General's store room. The menu was a handsome one - wines and liquors, white buscuit, raisins and other dried fruit, tongues, hams and beef. The Americans were soon enough "decently drunk" over the General's excellent Madeira wine. And so they lived like "hearty fellows" until the anchorage at Portsmouth, England - keeping suspicions down by snatching at the few scraps brought to them. The General, captain and the officers were astonished to find the prisoners "All brave and hearty. General Howe was heard to say "What, are none of them d—d Yankees sick! D—n them (says he) there is nothing but thunder and lightning will kill them!"

INTERROGATION ~ Once ashore, each prisoner faced a battery of detailed questions from two civil magistrates. The grilling was repeated and the answers compared. In this way, the British authorities hoped to ferret out any and all British subjects serving on American vessels. A noose would be their fate, while their American shipmates marched off to an indefinite confinement.

PRISONS

The men of the privateer "Angelica" were shortly on their way to Forten Prison - a dubious honor indeed! Located several miles from Portsmouth harbor at Gosport, it was originally built as a hospital for sick and wounded seamen in the days of Queen Anne. One hundred soldiers guarded the two large building. A sizable parade ground separated the two. Adjoining the prison was a large yard of three quarters of an acre, stockaded on all sides

LEG IRONS.

OLD MILL PRISON, ON A TONGUE OF LAND PROJECTING INTO THE SOUND, WAS NAMED AFTER WINDMILLS THAT STOOD ON THE SITE.

LONDON

SOUTHAMPTON

GOSPORT PORTSMOUTH

PLYMOUTH

FORTEN PRISON

and large enough to give the two hundred prisoners some degree of exercise. An open shed in the center was provided with seats for hot and sultry days.

A second place of confinement, the Old Mill Prison near Plymouth, made Forten seem like a luxury hotel. It wasn't Old Mill's hulking stone buildings, shut off from the outside world by two high walls. The hell of it could be summed up in two words by the four hundred prisoners ~ William Cowdray. As keeper of the prison, constant mischief spewed from his warped mind. For example, he bought hacks and necks of beef instead of the usual whole quarters. At that there were more maggots than meat. While pocketing the savings, he further reduced the meager allowance by boiling out the fat for tallow.

Much of the unappetizing remains was fed to his two hundred hogs, kept in a converted coal storage area, while most of his prisoners wasted away with hunger. To further line his pocket, he pilfered the money collected in the prisoners' charity box ~ and robbed those who still had a shilling or two still in their possession. It is interesting to note that the villainous Cowdray, fearful of repercussions at the end of the war, circulated a paper for signing. In effect, it stated that he had treated the Americans with kindness! The paper was promptly torn to shreds!

PRISONER ACTIVITIES ~ INCLUDING ESCAPE!

Regular schools were set up by the prisoners to teach reading, writing, arithmetic and navigation. Thanks to this sharing of knowledge, many became captains of their own vessels upon returning to America. A number of French officers, confined with the Yankees, taught their native language. A small income could be realized by carving articles from wood such as boxes, ship models and ladles. And there was the usual scuttlebutt, diary writing, exercising in the yard at ball and quoits ~ and plotting escape!

The latter activity was above and away the most popular. Some went over the wall ~ others tunneled under it. There were those who walked out, free as the air, in British officers' uniforms. One ingenious fellow attempted to substitute himself in the coffin of a mate who had gone to his reward. Guards were bribed. Deals were made with the country folk thereabouts (many came to view the prisoners daily), and on Sunday there might be upward to a thousand spectators. After helping with an escape, the man would be "recaptured" as part of the plot, then the five pounds reward

"CAT"

was divided between the two schemers. This profitable enterprize was actually worked fifteen times by several of the inmates.

Ingenuity and daring made the old records exciting indeed! Nathaniel Fanning told of a monumental excavation project. Tunneling left tell-tale dirt and stones that must be hidden. The work began at eleven o'clock at night and lasted until three o'clock each morning. Small canvas bags were used to carry the diggings to an old set of fireplaces in one of the buildings. Previously stopped up and white-washed, they were reopened and stuffed with dirt. A piece of white paper was pasted over the hole when each night's work was done. When a new dumping ground was needed, a hole was made through the ceiling to the roof—just large enough for a man to wiggle through. Several cart-loads were deposited before the hole was finally camouflaged with another piece of pasted paper.

Fragmentary reports point up a surprising number of escapes. During the years of 1779 and 1780 alone, some two hundred and thirteen men took their liberty from Forten and Mill prisons. But for those recaptured, it was forty days and nights in the "black hole" on bread and water. Even so, there were those who dug their way out of this isolated dungeon and made good their escape to France. Recaptured prisoners could count on being listed in the agent's books as deserters, and were not to be exchanged until the very last.

EXCHANGES
~ Escapees, safely on French soil, found that they could still help their emprisoned countrymen. Ben Franklin, not one for idleness, had organized a few privateering vessels to plague the English coastline. As chief negotiator for prisoners, Franklin developed more bargaining muscle as his list of British prisoners increased. There were setbacks aplenty, but finally an agreement for prisoner exchange became a reality.

INDEPENDENCE DAY CELEBRATION~
There seemed little to celebrate in the Old Mill. But in 1778, two years after the Declaration Of Independence in America, the prisoners marked the day with paper cockades. Half moon in shape with a background of thirteen stripes and a union with thirteen stars, each had INDEPENDENCE boldly printed in capital letters at the top. Across the bottom read "LIBERTY OR DEATH" or some appeal to heaven. Prison agents viewed such hat dressing with alarm—a double sentry was

CONJECTURAL REPRESENTATION OF COCKADE.

posted at the gate. But contrary to expectations, the Americans drew up in thirteen divisions. Each gave a rousing three cheers until the last division was reached. Then every man cheered as one. It was reported that every man kept his "colors hoisted 'til sunset".

BRITISH CURIOSITY AND KINDNESS
~ While cruelty could be expected from the military, the American mariners were showered with both curiosity and kindness by the average English citizen. In December 1776 the brig Dolton was taken by the British man of war "Reasonable"(64 guns). After docking at Plymouth, England, a number of British seamens' wives came aboard. When told that American prisoners were aboard, they asked "Are they white? Can they talk?" When the Yankee seamen were pointed out, they exclaimed "Why! they look like our people, and they talk English."!

Throughout England, rich and poor alike contributed to the welfare of the prisoners. By early 1778, for example, a husky £7000 sterling had been raised. At the Old Mill, each man received a great coat, a suit of clothes, two shirts, two pair of stockings, one pair of shoes, a jacket, as well as added rations from the efforts of these good people. Many visitors to the prisons brought books. Some, such as a minister by the name of Wren, took a more active and dangerous role on behalf of the prisoners. Mr. Wren harbored escapees from Forten Prison, then gave them clothes and money - and a safe journey to London. Once lost in its bustling streets, the Americans could easily gain passage to France by way of Dover and Ostend.

PRISON SHIPS

Should a privateer have the ill fortune to be taken in her own waters, the hulks of Wallabout Bay awaited. Once the pride of His Majesty's fleet, the derelict ships off Brooklyn, New York, had been stripped of their fittings. Gun ports had been nailed securely. The old transport Whitby was the first, and by October 1776 she was filled with rebel seamen. Among their considerable numbers was the prize crew from the Connecticut schooner "Spy", captured while bringing home the British prize ship "Hope".

THE PRISON SHIP JERSEY,
FORMERLY A 64 GUN SHIP
OF THE LINE.

The seamen of the "Spy" wrote the following letter of appeal, which, in part, revealed their distress aboard - (the appeal was successful, and shortly after, the men from the "Spy" had gained their freedom). It was dated December 9th 1776.

"There are more than two Hundred and fifty prisoners of us on board this ship (some of which are Sick and without the least assistance from Physician, Drugg, or Medicine) all fed on two-thirds allowance of Salt provisions and all crowded promiscuously together, without Distinction or Respect to Person Office or Colour, in the Small Room of a Ship's Between Decks, allowed only to walk the main deck from about Sun Rising till Sun Sett, at which time we are ordered below deck and suffered only one at once to come on deck to do what nature requires, and sometimes we have been even Denied that, and been obliged to make use of tubbs and bucketts below deck to the great offence of every Delicate Cleanly person as well as to great prejudice of all our healths. These

Sir with many other Miserable Circumstances too lengthy and too tedious to enumerate, are the just portraits of our present Situation. In short, sir, we have no prospect before our eyes but a kind of lingering inevitable death unless we obtain a timely and Seasonable Release."

By May of 1777, the "Whitby" had been replaced by several more converted ships. Five months later one burned to the water's edge, ending the lives and misery of an unknown number of Americans aboard. The second vessel went up in flames in February of 1778. Rumor had it that the prisoners were responsible, but none could deny that it was an effective means of ridding these sickly ships of their vermin. The prisoners were distributed among those British naval vessels wintering in the bay until more ships could be degraded to prison duty. One such, the "Jersey", claimed the dubious title of "Hell Afloat". Its stripped and wormy hull was perforated with two rows of barred holes, twenty inches square and ten feet apart. They defied escape as did the ten foot barrier that separated the British crew in the quarter deck from the main deck. Ladders from two doors connected the two levels. The wooden wall was punctured with multiple gun ports, should the Americans take it into the heads to change their status aboard.

Boredom weighed heavily until the 9:00 o'clock morning bell sounded. A representative of each six man mess hurried forward when his number was called. He received the vegetable and butter-free ration for the day. Usually the rancid, maggoty offering wasn't worth the effort. Then, for the remainder of the daylight hours, the men paced the deck for whatever exercise the crowding would permit. (There were often more than one thousand American seamen on board at a time!) At sundown, the men returned to the dank and filthy hold. Gratings secured the hatches, the guards took up stations there, and another long night had begun.

There were mighty few escape attempts from men broken by starvation and disease. Death took no holidays — shortly after peace was declared, it was estimated that almost eleven thousand died on the "Jersey" alone. Countless patriots were buried along the Wallabout beaches, resting in a different sort

EAST RIVER

NEW YORK

JERSEY

BROOKLYN

WALLABOUT BAY

† = GRAVES.

SECTION OF A MOORING CHAIN USED BY A BRITISH PRISON SHIP IN NEW YORK HARBOR. 1776 — 1783. DRAWN HALF SIZED.

of peace than that for which they had fought.

AND MORE PRISONS~

Prisons in more permanent British possession than New York included Halifax in
Nova Scotia, Antigua in the Leeward
Islands, and the Island of Jamaica. The
"Spanish Town Papers" have highlighted the
plight of those arriving in the last-named
colony. Letters and documents, taken from
the captured privateers, show that impress-
ment gangs in Kingston helped ease the
crowded prisons. Among the papers of the
Charleston schooner "Martha and Mary"
captured by the H.M.S. Hind, was the
following~

SNUFF BOX, MADE BY AN AMERICAN
PRISONER ABOARD THE "JERSEY".
DRAWN TWICE THE SIZE.

"7 April 1777
Mr. Singer living in Kingstone:
Dear Sir,
    This comes to Acquaint you that I am on board the
Hind 20 guns ship I was press't that Minuit I went out of
Youre House But with the Blessing of god I shall have the
pleasure of seeing you a gain in a short time. I would be
obliged to you to Look after my prize money my Respects
to your wife,
                    Wm. Blanchard "

Not all ship's papers were so handily taken by the
King's Navy. The Baltimore brig "Nancy" never reached the
port of Curaçao in 1779. When the H.M.S. "Sparrow" hove
her to the "Nancy's" captain threw the incriminating
ship's papers over the side. None-the-less, she was taken
into Port Royal as a suspicious vessel. Before the
trial, Acting-Lieutenant Fitton was shark fishing aboard
another British ship off distant Jeremel. The stomach
of his catch held the "Nancy's" papers, all neatly tied
and, unfortunately, still quite legible. The papers
were hurried to the Vice-Admiralty court in Jamaica,
and the "Nancy" was condemned in due course.

INK HORN.
THE TOP
UNSCREWS
TO RELEASE
A PEN.

CAPTURED BRITISH SEAMEN, by contrast,
could expect humane treatment in the hands of
the Americans. A search through old papers and
records has failed to show any evidence to the contrary. Such compassion is all the more remarkable when
one remembers the years under a heavy-handed king and their
treatment as "rebels and traitors". Perhaps this explains, in part, a willing-
ness to ship aboard a Yankee privateersman, when hanging would be the
fate if captured.
    For example, early in 1782, the privately armed sloop "Lively"
(Captain D. Adams commanding) rescued the shipwrecked crew of the
British frigate "Blonde". Every assistance was given the survivors,
and the castaways were brought safely into port.

PRIVATEERING JACKS OF ALL TRADES

Not all privateer engagements were on the high seas. For example, one of the fastest sailers in New England, the "General Putnam" (20 nine pounders and 150 men, Captain Harmon commanding) had taken fourteen prizes earlier in the war. Her fleetness was of little use, however, when she was driven into a harbor near present day Saco by a frigate. The Britisher came to anchor to wait out her quarry. Not one to collect barnacles in port, Captain Harmon hauled one of his guns ashore and up to a point of land. The frigate was fired upon, and the warship answered with whole broadsides. But before the woods could be leveled by British cannon balls, the American gun cut away the other's fore-stay. She was obliged to come to sail and put to sea.

Down the coast, the tiny boat "Speedwell" (2 guns and twenty men, Captain Levi Barlow commanding) was forced into Nantucket harbor "by a privateer schooner of superior force manned by Tory refugees and sheep-stealers from New York..." The Independent Chronicle of July 25, 1782 went on to say that Barlow and his crew landed by a wharf. There they hove up a breastwork and made ready for attack. But an assault came from an unexpected quarter when they were driven off by some less-than-patriotic islanders. These people had profited from their trading with the enemy, and had little affection for Captain Barlow (he had recently taken a number of their kind prisoners).

While the Tory privateer made splinters of the "Speedwell", Barlow and his men made their way to the Massachusetts mainland and held a hurried meeting with Captain Lot Dimmick of Falmouth. Several small boats were borrowed, and the two captains and a part of their crews made way for Nantucket. The enemy vessel still lazed off the island. Commandeering a sloop at anchor, the Yankees sailed into a warm welcome from swivels and musketry, but were able to board and take the vessel. The twenty-eight prisoners were taken to the friendlier port of Falmouth.

Commando-like raids on British towns was no rarity. As reported by the Boston Gazette on September 24, 1781, the schooner "Resolution" (6 guns, 25 men, Captain William Morgan commanding), in company with Captain Curtiss of the schooner "Reprisal", attacked the town of Annapolis Royal. The fort, which "consisted of nine 18 and 9 pounders", was destroyed, and the entire garrison made prisoners. The governor was among those taken, and with this bonus, an exchange was made for the recently captured privateer captain of the "Resolution."

Again Nova Scotia was the target when the schooner "Hero" (9 guns, 25 men, Captain Babcock commanding) along with Captain Stoddard of the "Scammel", Woodbury of the "Hope", and Tibbetts of the "Swallow", landed ten leagues below Halifax. Objective - take the town of Lunenburg, two miles to the north. According to the Boston Gazette of July 15, 1782, ninety seamen under Lieutenant Barteman waded through heavy musket fire and burned the commanding officer's quarters and a blockhouse in the northwest part of town. The garrison retreated to the south blockhouse where they returned a brisk fire. Their enthusiasm ended when the Americans closed the contest with a few balls from a four-pounder cannon.

Care was taken to observe "the strictest Decorum" toward the civilians, and their clothing and furniture" inviolably preserved for their use." The Royal magazine was stored in the hold of the "Scammel" along with quantities of "Dry Goods, twenty Puncheons of Good West-India Rum, and the King's Beef, Pork and Flour." Other cargo included the British colonel and some of the principal citizens, and the town was ransomed for a thousand pounds sterling. "On the Side of the brave Sons of Liberty, three were wounded slightly, one dangerously; on the Part of the Abettors of Oppression and Despotism, the Number of slain and wounded unknown, only one of their Slain being found."

CAPT JAMES MUGFORD.

On May 19, 1776, the privateer "Lady Washington" (4 guns, 6 crew, Captain Joseph Cunningham commanding) and the schooner "Franklin" (several 2 pounders and swivels, 21 men, Captain James Mugford commanding) sailed from Boston Harbor. Their departure was duly noted by enemy shipping. When the "Franklin" ran aground in the "Gut", thirteen or more British boats-many with swivels - and two hundred marines and sailors pushed off under cover of darkness. Between nine and ten o'clock, the "Lady Washington", anchored near the "Franklin", discovered the raiding party. Challenged, they shouted back that they were from Boston. Captain Mugford immediately fired. His crew followed with a volley. By cutting the cable, the "Franklin" was able to bring a broadside to bear. The charges, loaded with musket balls, cut into the enemy. Before the cannon could be reloaded, two or three of the boats were alongside. Within minutes there were eight or nine boatloads attempting to board, but the attack was repulsed with muskets and boarding pikes. Two boats were sunk with no survivors.

Meanwhile, the "Lady Washington" was set upon by the remaining four or five boats. Captain Cunningham and his six men, with their swivels, blunderbusses and muskets were able to drive off the British. But there was no celebration that night. Captain Mugford had met his death by a musket ball.

REFITTING IN PORT

Refitting and repairs were a never-ending chore aboard wooden vessels. When away from American waters, there were some favorite ports of call for the privateersmen. The town of Morlaix in France was one such, snugly located some five miles from the English Channel. To it ran a river, blest with a hard, gravelly bottom. A ship of three hundred tons could lay along the keys, safe from heavy winds. At low water a ship would be left largely aground. Nature thereby helped the sailor with his "graving"- or scrubbing- of the ship's bottom to make it swift-sailing again.

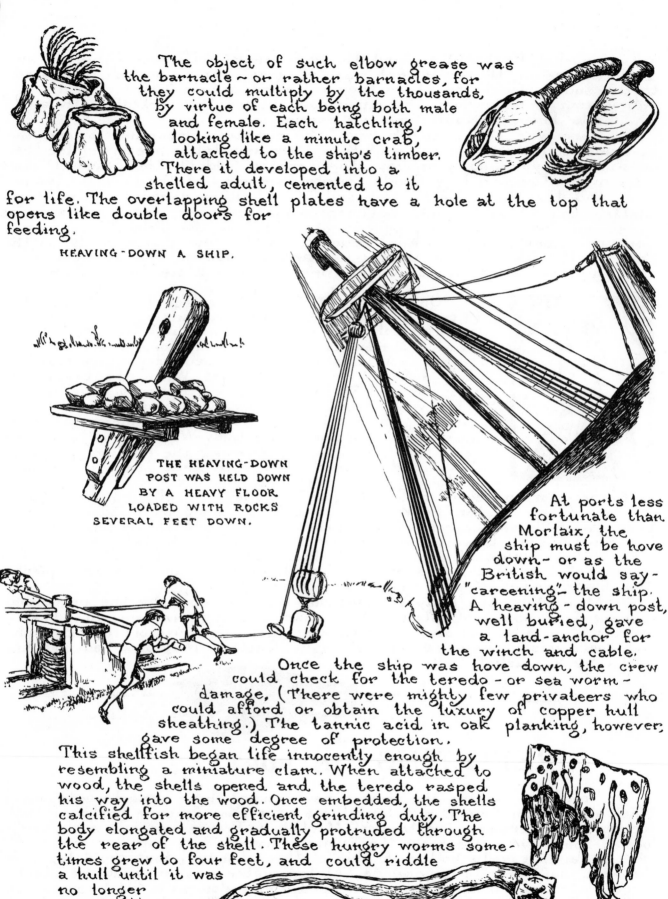

The object of such elbow grease was the barnacle ~ or rather barnacles, for they could multiply by the thousands, by virtue of each being both male and female. Each hatchling, looking like a minute crab, attached to the ship's timber. There it developed into a shelled adult, cemented to it for life. The overlapping shell plates have a hole at the top that opens like double doors for feeding.

HEAVING-DOWN A SHIP.

THE HEAVING-DOWN POST WAS HELD DOWN BY A HEAVY FLOOR LOADED WITH ROCKS SEVERAL FEET DOWN.

At ports less fortunate than Morlaix, the ship must be hove down ~ or as the British would say ~ "careening" the ship. A heaving-down post, well buried, gave a land-anchor for the winch and cable.

Once the ship was hove down, the crew could check for the teredo ~ or sea worm ~ damage. (There were mighty few privateers who could afford or obtain the luxury of copper hull sheathing.) The tannic acid in oak planking, however, gave some degree of protection.

This shellfish began life innocently enough by resembling a miniature clam. When attached to wood, the shells opened and the teredo rasped his way into the wood. Once embedded, the shells calcified for more efficient grinding duty. The body elongated and gradually protruded through the rear of the shell. These hungry worms sometimes grew to four feet, and could riddle a hull until it was no longer sea-worthy.

PORTS AND PRIZES

There were other favored privateering refitting ports. Brest, France, with seven fathoms of water, and Bilbao, Spain, where Jonathan Haraden mauled the "Archilles", were among them. And there was the Dutch port of St. Eustatius in the Leeward Islands, not only noted for refitting but also a reshipping center for half of the French arms and ammunition slated for the American colonies.

To the seaman, these foreign ports also meant shore leave - and perhaps an advance in pay to make it memorable. The French were fond indeed of the "Bostonian" - as all Americans in that country were called. Where the French ladies were concerned, it boarded on adoration - in no way objectionable to the Yankee visitor. The Spanish, however, had more love for foreign money than the wild singing down the crooked streets, or dispatching great quantities of wine in the local shops. As early as the Autumn of 1776 there were nineteen American privateers in the port of Bilbao, and the locals had to admit that business was good.

In these distant ports, the privateer could dispose of his prize vessels. Many of the ship owners had stationed agents to pay out money on account. In the United States, the disposal of prize vessels was a well defined procedure. Fifteen days before the trial was due, the notification of the sale with the name of ship, description, and the date of the trial was published in the local newspapers. Owners of the vessel or those otherwise concerned could appear and present any reason why the prize should not be condemned and sold. No more than twelve jurors heard the evidence in the Court of Justice. If the vessel was proved a prize and properly taken under the "Articles", it was sold.

The trial charges and sale costs took the first bite from the sale profits. Of the remaining, not less than a fourth and not more than a third was divided among those making the capture. The privateer ship owners received the rest. However, if a prize were captured after being condemned in an enemy court, the sale money would go to the captors alone.

The privateer profits and distress to the enemy shipping were staggering. Captain Abraham Whipple of Rhode Island may well have captured more British vessels than any other during the Revolution. On a single cruise, his privateer took twenty-three prizes valued at one million dollars. In 1779, Captain Whipple combined the talents of his scrappy "Providence" with Captain John Rathbourne's "Queen of France" and Captain William Simpkins "Ranger". In several weeks, the trio had taken eight prize merchantmen into Boston ~ the value was in excess of a million dollars. A fourteen year old lad on the "Ranger", fresh from the farm less than a month, received as his share twenty pounds of cotton, a like quantity of all-spice, ginger and logwood, one ton of sugar, between thirty and forty gallons of fourth proof Jamaica rum AND seven hundred dollars.

CAPT ABRAHAM WHIPPLE.

Selling one's share of prize goods took a bit of Yankee know-how. Continental currency depreciated daily, and months at sea could keep a man out of touch with current values. For example, one Jonathan Chapman sold forty bushels of his prize salt for eighty dollars a bushel. Three thousand, two hundred Continental dollars might seem like a fortune, but in a few weeks, this sum might not buy back a single bushel. Land, houses, or shops kept their value, and many a privateersman with foresight could invest in real estate - and perhaps his own business.

Privateering was a gamble, and as with any gamble, there were winners and losers. The young American nation could only profit from these enterprising privately armed vessels. No citizen was out of pocket when one was built or purchased, outfitted and supplied, or captured or sunk. At no cost, the country had a fleet of ships that was a tolerable substitute for the tiny Continental Navy, would bring back war booty for the army, and be a proving ground for those officers and men who would later enter the naval service.

The British were the losers in this private sea war. Their Restrictive Trade Acts, earlier designed to restrain the ambitious Yankee traders, had backfired. No port or body of water was safe from their hit-and-run attacks. Cargo vessels were taken in such great numbers that insurance rates were doubled - then reportedly rose to thirty percent when sailing under a strong escort. Without escort, the cost rose to fifty percent. The British merchants brought heavy pressure on Parliament for a rapid return to peace. And when American independence was at last a reality, the privateer could take a degree of credit for the outcome. Hopefully, history will give these daring patriots their due.

OFFICER - FROM AN ENGRAVING BY PAUL REVERE FOR A 1775 MASS^{TTS} TREASURY NOTE.

Index

(Note: Page numbers in italic type refer to illustrations.)

A

Activities in prison 83
Adams, Captain D. 87
"Adventure", privateer brig 57
Adze, felling *11*, 11
Altitude scale, quadrant *59*
Anchor cable 36
"Andromeda", British frigate 81
"Angelica", privateer brig 81
Annapolis Royal, Nova Scotia, attack on 88
Antigua, Leeward Islands 87
"Archilles", British privateer 67, 75
Armament of "Spider Catchers" 8
Articles of Agreement 31, 91
   captain's instructions 31
   officers' and crew's duties 31
   rewards and punishments 31
   share proportions 31
   ship owner's instructions 31
Axe, broad *11*, 11
Axe, felling, *11*, 11
Axemen 11

B

Babcock, Captain 88
Baggage, taken from Americans 81
Bailey, Jacob, his record of journey
   35, 39, 40
Ballast *42*, 42
Baltimore, Maryland, brig from 87
Barges, privateering 8
Barlow, Captain Levi 88
Barnacles *90*, 90
Barney, Captain Joshua 71
Bar shot 46
Barteman, Lieutenant, as leader of raid 88
Battle preparations
   American rifle *70*, 71
   battle rattle 68
   British sea-service musket 70
   carpenter 69
   cohorn *70*
   cook 69
   fire bucket *69*
   firemen 69
   gun crews 68
   hand grenade *70*
   main-top *70*, 71
   marines 69
   officer's pewter whistle *68*
   pike-head *69*
   powder boys 69
   privateer sword *69*
   quarter gunners 69
   ship's arms chest *70*
   stink pot *71*
   topmen 69, *70*
Belaying pin *19*
Bells, for time on board 38
Bells, ship's *38*
"Betsey", privateer brig 57
Beverly, Massachusetts, first mill
   for manufacturing sail cloth in 20
Bilboa Harbor, Bay of Biscay, Spain 67, 68
Bits, spoon or dowel 12
"Bittacle" *64*
Bitt, hoisting anchor *36*
Blanchard, William, letter from 87
Block and tackle *19*, 19
   block, fiddle *19*
   double shiv *19*
   pin *19*
   shell *19*
   single shiv *19*
   stay lashing *35*
   tackle, cannon-training *44*, 47
   work advantage *19*, 19
"Blonde", British frigate 87
Bluff 68
Blunderbusses 75, 89
Boarding
   boarding enemy at anchor
     against wind *74*, 74
   boarding to leeward *74*, 74
   boarding to windward *73*, 73
   boat hook 75
   British boarding axe 75
   British boarding pistol 75
   Bucks County sharpshooters 71
   calculated collisions 71
   grappling *72*
   how to board 73

   pinching *73*, 73
   privateer blunderbuss 75
   running *73*, 73
   three adventures in 75
Boats, hoisting aboard *35*, 35
Boltrope 21
Bonds 26
"Boston", Continental frigate 58
Boston Gazette
   Dec. 9, 1776 80
   Nov. 13, 1780 29
   Sept. 24, 1781 88
   July 15, 1782 88
Boston harbor 89, 91
"Bostonian", French name for Americans 91
Bo'sun's pipe 34
Bow, sharp 9
Bowsprit sails *22*
Braces *18*
Brewster, Captain 76
Brigantine *22*
Brig (vessel) *22*
Brig (ship's jail), location of *40*, 42
"Bristol", H.M.S., capture of
   signals of 57
British Navy
   convoy duty 58
   figureheads *54*, 54, *55*, 55
   Regulations of 1790 50
   rum ration 51
Broad arrow 14
Broad arrow tree mark *14*
Brooklyn, New York 85
Bulwarks, pierced for cannon 8
Buntlines *24*

C

Cable 36, 41
Cable crisis 38
Cable hatch 36, *37*
"Calls" on bo'sun's pipes 34
Candle holder *40*
Cannabis sativa (plant) 15
Cannister, for shot 46
Cannon, ships'
   accuracy 45
   below deck 40
   breeching rope *44*
   carronade *46*, 46
   cartridges *47*, 48
   compared to land cannon 44
   copper knife *48*
   drill 44
   eyebolts *44*, *47*, 47
   firing 49
     at will 45
   foundries 45
   gun port *47*, 48
   handspike 44
   instructions for gunners 47
   lack of 45
   linstock 49
   loading *47*, 47, *48*, 48, *49*, 49
   pick *47*
   powder barrel *47*
   powder measure *48*
   privateer "Nancy", from *44*
   projectiles 45
   "Quakers" 46
   quoin *49*
   rammer *48*
   recoil 10
   side tackle *44*, 44
   sighting 45
   size 9, 44
   speed of loading 45
   sponger *48*
   storage of shot and ball 41
   swivel gun 49, *50*, 50
   tackle for *44*, 44
   tampion *47*
   training tackle *44*, 44, 47
   windage 45
   worming iron *49*
Canvas, gun port cover 68
Cape Trafalgar battle,
   Nelson's death during 51
Capstan *36*, 36, *37*, 37
Capstan chanties 53
Captain
   authority of 27, 28

   education of 28
   navigational equipment of 65
   qualifications of 25
   qualities of 27, 28
   patriotism of 28
   reputation of 29
   role of, in selecting crew 29
   role of, in selecting officers 30
   speaking trumpet of *34*, 34
Care of wounded 78, 79
Cargo ships, European 8
Carnes, Captain John 25
Carpenter, battle preparations of 69
Carronade *46*, 46
Carron, Scottish foundries in 46
Cartridges, cannon *47*, 47, *48*, 48
Carvings, stern 13
Casks, meat and water 41, *42*, 42
"Cassandra", privateer schooner 57
Castaways, British 87
"Cat" *83*
Cathead, U.S.S. "Constitution" *37*
Catting the anchor 37
Caulking *12*, 12
Caulking hammer *12*
Chafing gear *77*
Chain shot *46*
Channel *17*
Chanteyman 53
Chanties
   double-pull 53
   single-pull 53
   windlass or capstan 53
Charleston, South Carolina,
   schooner from 57, 87
Charts 65
Chase
   closing to windward *67*, 67
   failing wind *67*, 67
   scudding *67*, 67
   to determine speed of enemy *66*, 66
   to leeward *66*, 66
   to windward *66*, 66
Chesapeake Bay 8, 9
Chesapeake swift vessels 9
Chest, Captain Benjamin Cox's 28
Chest, ship's arms 70
Clam rake *52*
Clews, of square sail *22*
Cockade, Independence Day celebration *84*
Coffin of Captain James Mugford *89*
Cohorn 70
Colors and signals 56, 80
   British merchantman flag *56*
   disadvantages of 57
   flying false flags 56
   lone-wolfing 57
   privateers' and merchantmen's flag *56*
   "ruse de guerre" 56
   signals, variety of 57
Colors, hull 13
Commando-like raids 88
Commission, privateering 25, 26
Compass and sun dial, pocket *60*
Concern for civilians 89
Condemned American vessels 87
Congress, commissions issued by 25
"Congress", privateer 75, 76
"Constitution", U.S.S., cathead from *37*
Continental Army
   benefits received from
     privateering 7, 92
   soldiers aboard privateer 76
   surgeon turned privateersman 80
Continental cruisers 7
Continental currency, depreciation of 92
Continental Navy
   officers for 28
   privateering a substitute for 92
Contributions for American prisoners 85
Convoys, British
   formation of 58
   great numbers of merchantmen in 58
   privateer attacks on 58
   sailing of an open secret 58
   weather advantage of 58
Cook, battle preparations of 69
Copper sheathing 13, 90
Course by compass *63*, 63
Cowdray, William
   (villainous prison keeper), 83
Crew
   chosen by captain 29
   clothing of
     bell-bottom trousers *32*, 32
     hats *32*, 32
     neckerchief *32*, 32
     peacoat *32*, 32
     queues *32*, 32

Crew (cont.)
   foreign volunteers in 30
   living arrangements of
      hammocks 42, *43*, 43
      head 43
      quarters 8, 40, 42, 43
      tables *43*
   officers of 30
   outsized, on privateer 10
   prize crew 30
   seamen in 30
   topmen, advice for 38
Crowbars, fired by cannon 75
Cruises, short 9
Cunningham, Captain Joseph 89
Curaçao, port of 87
Curiosity of British citizens 84
Cutlass, light seaman's *28*
   use in boarding 76

D

Dead American prisoners 86
Deadeyes *16*
Deadrise, hull 9
"Deane", privateer ship 29
Deck gear 40
Decks, reinforced 8
Deck stopper, used in weighing anchor *36*
Deduction, finding position by
   "bittacle" *64*
   course by compass *63*, 63
   deep-sea-lead ("dipsey") 62, *62*, 63
   dog vane *64*
   fathoms 62
   half minute glass 61, *61*, 62
   hand-lead *62*
   "heaving the lead" *62*, 62
   hours 61
   knots per hour 61
   leeway 64, *65*, 65
   log *61*, 61
   log board *61*, 61
   log book 61
   log line *61*, 61
   markings or "deeps" *63*
   winds 69
Delaware River 71
Dennis, Captain William 81
Derby, Elias *25*, 25
Derby Wharf, Salem, Massachusetts *25*, 25
Diet, see Victuals
Dimmick, Captain Lot 88
Ditty bag *33*
   construction *33*
   contents
      jackknife *33*
      razor *33*
      scissors *33*
      shaving brush *33*
      shaving dish *33*
Ditty box and contents *33*
Dividers, American *65*
Dog vane *64*
Dover, England 85
Dried vegetables *51*, 51
Drinking
   daily ration 51
   drunkenness, classifications of 51
   "Nelson's blood" 51
   pewter mug *51*
   rum 51
Drowne, Dr. Solomon 43, 80
Dubbers 11, *12*, 12
Duel, aborted 28

E

Eelskins, for covering queue *32*, 32
Egg Harbor 8, 80
Escapes by American prisoners 83, 84, 85
Exchange of prisoners 84

F

Falmouth, Massachusetts 88
Fanning, Nathaniel,
   account of capture 81, 84
Fathoms 62
Fid *20*
Fiddle block *19*
Figureheads
   British and French *54*, 54, 55
   early Egyptian 54
   English beast carving *54*
   from privateer "Jolly Tar" *55*
   privateering 55
   "Royal George", H.M.S., injury to 55
   superstitions about 54
Fire bucket 69
Fire fighting instructions 76

Firemen, battle preparations of 69
Fisher, Dr. Joshua, medicine chest of *79*
Fish hooks and hitch *52*
"Fishing" cracked spars 77
Fishing the anchor 37
Fitton, Acting-Lieutenant 87
Food, see Victuals
Fore-and-aft sails *21*, 21, 22, 22
Fork, from H.M.S. "Augusta" *51*
Forten Prison, Gosport, England 82, 83, 84
Foundry, Carron, Scotland 46
"Frame-up!" *11*, 11
Framing the hull *11*, 11
Franklin, Benjamin, role of in
   speeding prisoner exchange 84
"Franklin", schooner 89
Freeboard, American differences in 9
   decreased 9
French arms reshipping center,
   St. Eustatius 91
Furled sail *22*, 24, 24

G

Gamble of privateering 25
Gammoning *17*
Gasket *17*
Gauge, wooden shot *45*
Gauge, wrought iron *45*
Geddes, Captain George 75
"General Monk", captured
   American privateer 71
"General Pickering", privateer 67, 68, 69
"General Putnam", privateer 88
"General Washington", privateer 71
"Gentlemen Volunteers" 30
Glass, half minute 61, *61*, *62*, 62
Glass, hanging half hour 38
"Golden Eagle", British brig 68
Goods, used to purchase ships 10
Gosport, England 82
Grape shot *46*
"Graving" or scrubbing 89
Grease horn *15*
Grenade, hand *70*
Grog, see Rum
Gunners, instructions for
   aim *47*
   cast off lashings *47*, 47
   clear touch-hole *47*, 47
   fire *47*, 47
   haul in gun *47*, 47
   hoist powder *47*
   judge wind *47*
   prime *47*, 47
   raise gun-port *47*, 47
   ram ball *47*, 47
   ram powder *47*, 47
   ram wadding *47*, 47
   ready for battle 68
   run carriage forward 47
   sponge *47*, 47
   swab *47*

H

Hadley's reflecting quadrant
   altitude scale *59*
   colored glasses *59*
   horizon glass *59*, 60
   index *59*
   index glass *59*, 60
   sight vane *59*, 60
   vernier *59*
Halifax, Nova Scotia 87
Halliards *18*
Hammock nettings and stowage *43*
"Hancock", Continental frigate 58
Handcuffs *81*
Hand-lead *62*
Handspike, use of in training cannon *49*
"Happy Return", snow, sale of in Boston 46
Haraden, Captain Jonathan 67, *68*, 75, 91
Hard tack 51
   recipe for 51
Harmon, Captain 88
Hats, crew
   brim variations *32*
   sailor's flat-brimmed *32*
   three-cornered *32*
   wide-brimmed *32*
Hawsepipes 37
Hawsing iron *12*
Headroom below decks 30
Heaving down post *90*
"Heaving the lead" *62*, 62
"Heaving the log" *61*, 61
"Hell Afloat" 86
Hemp *15*, 15
"Hero", schooner 88

Hewing *11*, 11
   spars *14*, 14
Hill, Captain Hugh 27, 28
"Hind", H.M.S. 35, 87
Hoisting boats aboard 35
Hoisting sale *22*, 22, *24*, 24
Holystone 77
"Hope", British prize ship 85
"Hope", privateer 37, 80
Horizon glass, quadrant *59*, 60
Hove down, procedure 90
Hubbell, Captain Amos 76
Hull
   average size 9
   berth deck *40*
   brig *40*
   construction 10, *10*, 11, *11*, 12, *12*
   cost 10
   forecastle *40*
   fore hatch *40*
   galley *40*
   head *40*
   hold *40*
   main hatch *40*
   main or gun deck *40*
   quarterdeck *40*
   quarters, officers and crew *40*
   pumps *40*
   remodeled for privateering 8
   "sharp" American 9, *9*
   typical privateer *9*, *40*, 41, 42, 43
   weight placement in 10

I

"Idlers" 39
Independence Day celebration 84
Independent Chronicle, July 25, 1782 88
Index, quadrant *59*
Inflation in ship building 10
Inflation, prize money 92
Ink horn *87*
Instructions to privateers 26
Insurance, rising costs of British 92
Interrogation of American prisoners 82
Investment, prize money 92
Investors 10, 25
Irons, leg *80*
   British prisoners in 80

J

Jackknife *33*
"Jason", privateer 72
"Jersey", prison ship *85*, 85
Jibs *22*
Johnson, Captain Henry 80
"Jolly Tar" figureheads *55*
Jug, pewter thunder *41*
"Julius Caesar", privateer sloop 76
Jury mast and lashing *77*

K

Keel construction 11
Keel, scarfed *11*
Kindness of British citizens 84
Kindness to British prisoners 80
Kingston, Jamaica 87
Knives
   draw *14*
   gunner's *47*
   jackknife *33*
   points broken for safety *52*
   rigger's *15*
   sailmaker's *20*
   sailor's *52*
   table, from H.M.S. "Augusta" *51*
Knots per hour 61

L

"Lady Washington", privateer 89
Lake Champlain, gunboat
   "Philadelphia" on *12*
Lamp soot, for darkening designs *52*
Landlubbers 29
Langrage projectiles *46*
Lantern, cabin *40*
Lanthorns, for lighting 40
Lanyard, rigging *16*
Lashing, small boat 35
Lays (rope twists) *15*
Leaks, stopping *76*, 76
Leeway 64, *65*, 65
Leg iron *82*
Letter of appeal from American prisoners 85
Letter of Marque 25
Lifts *18*
Light, below decks 40
Linstock *49*
"Lively", privateer 87

Loading cannon 47, 47, 48, 48, 49, 49
Lobscouse, a favorite meal 51
Loft, rope and sail 10
Log board 61
Log book 61
Log line 61
Long Island Sound 8, 76
Longitude, determination of 60
Loops ("cringles") 22
L'Orient, France 27
Lunenburg, Nova Scotia 88

M

Magazine, fire protection 76
Magazine, in converted privateers 8
Main-top battle preparations 70, 71
Making irons, for caulking 12
"Manly", a favorite song 53
Manly, Captain John 72
Maps
    English prisons 83
    seacoast, Nova Scotia to Newport 88
    Wallabout Bay, New York 86
Marine guard 30
Marines, battle preparations of 69
Markings or "deeps" 63
"Marquis", privateer 57
"Martha and Mary", Charleston schooner 87
Massachusetts treasury note 92
Mast hoop 22
Mast, raked 9
Medical text symptoms 79
Medicine 78, 79
Medicine bottles 79
Medicine chest 79
Mercator's charts 65
Merchantmen
    American 9
    British swift-sailing 58
    European 8, 9
Meridian 59, 59
Messenger, use of in hoisting anchor 36
Mooring buoy 38
Mooring chain, from British prison ship 86
Morlaix, France 89
Mugford, Captain James 89, 89
Musket, British sea-service 70

N

"Nancy", brig from Baltimore 70
Nantucket 8
Nantucket harbor 88
"Nautical Almanack", use of 59
Nautical mile 59
Navigation, see Position at sea
Neckerchief 32
Needle holder 20
Needles 20, 21, 52
Nelson, Lord, instructions of,
    for painting gun ports 13
"Nelson's blood" 51
New England swift vessels 9
New Jersey coastline 8
New York Bay 8
New York City 8
"Nipper boys" 37
Norfolk, Virginia 55
North Atlantic, weather in 9

O

Oakum, for caulking 12, 12
Officer, from engraving by Paul Revere 92
Officers
    "idlers" 39
    qualities of 30
    quarters of 41
    rank 30
    sailing master 30
    station 30
    wardroom 41
Old Mill Prison 83, 84
Ostend, Belgium 85
Overboard, falling 39
"Oznabrig" linen 20
Oznaburg, Germany 20

P

Paint, hull 13
Parcelling, standing rigging 17
Parliament, pressure on 92
Parliament, role of in delaying
    trials of prisoners 81
Parral 18
Patriotism of captain 28

Pawls, capstan 37
"Paying", formula for hull 13
Peacoat 32
"Philadelphia", spoon and dowel bits
    from gunboat 12
Phipps, Captain 44
Pick, for cannon touch-hole 47
Pickled spars 14
Pike-head 69
Pikes, boarding 76
"Pilgrim", privateer 27
Pin, block 19
Pipe, bo'sun's 34
Pipe, sailor's smoking 52
Pistol, English naval 28
Pitch brush and disk 77
Pit saw 10, 11
Plane, use of in hull construction 12
Plankers 11, 12, 12
Planks for ship's skin 10, 10
Plymouth, England 83, 84
Poles, North and South 59
"Pooped" 67
Port, gun 47
Port Royal 87
Portsmouth, England 81
"Porus", privateer, weekly menu on 50
Position at sea
    charts 65, 65
    finding by deduction 61
    finding by observation 59
    Hadley's reflecting quadrant 59
    latitude 59, 59
    longitude 60, 60
    pocket compass and sun dial 60
Preservation of Admiral Nelson's body 51
Preserving meat 50
Pricker 20
Prisoners
    Americans treated as pirates 81
    British seamen, kind treatment of 87
    Dr. Solomon Drowne's account 80
    exchanges of, arranged by
        Benjamin Franklin 84
    handcuffs 81
    ingenuity of 84
    interrogation of Americans 82
    kindness of Americans 87
    leg iron 80
    mistreatment in prison 83
    Nathaniel Fanning's account 81
    stealing from 81
Prisons
    activities in 83
    Antigua, Leeward Islands 87
    "Black Hole" 84
    "cat" 83
    English, map of 83
    escape from 83, 84
    Forten Prison,
        Gosport, England 82, 83, 84
    Halifax, Nova Scotia 87
    impressment as relief for
        crowded conditions in 87
    Independence Day celebration in 84
    Kingston, Jamaica 87
    Old Mill Prison,
        Plymouth, England 83, 84
    schools in 83
Prison ships
    British transport "Whitby" 85
    death aboard 86
    distress aboard 85
    escapes 86
    "Jersey" 85, 86
    letter of appeal by "Spy" crew 85
    mooring chain from 86
    rations 86
    snuff box, made aboard "Jersey" 87
    Wallabout Bay, graves on 86
Privateering
    advantages of over Navy service 29
    barges 8
    congressional commission for 7
    contributions 7
    conversion of ships to 8
    research sources 7
    scarcity of records 7
    sharp, swift vessels 8
    ship owners 7
    states' commissions 7
    total ships and prizes captured 7
    whaleboats 8, 8
Prize crew 58
Prize goods storage 9
Prizes captured
    from town of Lunenburg 89
    great numbers taken 91

in Articles of Agreement 31
inflation and investment 92
listed 80
means of disposal 91
military 28
use by seamen 30
Projectiles
    bar shot 46
    cannister, wood and metal 46
    chain shot 46
    grape shot 46
    langrage 46
    shot gauges 45
    solid shot 45
    wooden shoe or "sabot" 45
Protractor, British 65
"Providence", privateer 91
Provisions, storage of 41, 42
Pulling songs 53
Pump, location of 42
Punishments, authorized by
    articles of agreement 31
Purchase, ship 10

Q

Quadrant and box, Captain Hugh Hill's 27
Quadrant, Hadley's reflecting 59
Quarterdeck
    respect for 34
    steering from 34
Quarter-gunners, battle preparations of 69
"Queen of France", privateer 91
Queues
    four-strand square sinnet 32
    rattail 32
Quoin, cannon 49

R

Rake, clam 52
Rammer, cannon 48
"Randolph", privateer brig 57
"Ranger", privateer 91
Rathbourne, Captain John 91
Ratlines 17
Rattle, battle 68
Razor 33
"Reasonable", British man of war 84
Reefing sail 22, 22
Refitting and repairs
    barnacles 90, 90
    Bilbao, Spain 91
    Brest, France 91
    "graving" or scrubbing 89
    heaving down post 90
    hove down, to 90
    Morlaix, France 89
    St. Eustatius, Leeward Islands 91
    teredo or seaworm 90, 90
Religion 55
    call to quarters prayer 55, 56
Repairs
    chafing gear 77
    "fishing" cracked spars 77
    holystone 77
    jury mast and knot 77
    pitch brush and dish 77
    swab 77
"Reprisal", schooner 88
"Resolution", schooner 88
Restrictive Trade Acts 9
    backfiring of 92
Revere, Paul, engraving by 92
Rewards, authorized by
    articles of agreement 31
Rifle, accuracy of 71
    American 70, 70, 71
Rigging gear 15
    belt 15
    cutting technique 15, 15
    grease horn 15
    marlingspike 15
    rigger's knife 15
Rigging, running 18, 19
    belaying pin 19
    block and tackle 19, 19
    braces 18
    halliards 18
    lifts 18
Rigging, standing
    deadeyes 16
    gammoning 17
    lanyard, use of 17
    parcelling 17
    ratlines 17
    serving 17
    shrouds 16
    stays 16
    worming 17

Rig, topsail schooner 9
Rope
    cable-laid 15
    hawser-laid 15
    shroud-laid 15
    stitches 21
Royal Navy, convoy duty 9
"Royal Savage", swivel gun from 50
Rubber, seam 20, 21
Rum
    daily ration 51
    grog invitation, *Boston Gazette* 29
    "Nelson's blood" 51
    pewter mug, American 51

S

"Sabot" 45
Saco, Maine, present-day 88
Sailmaker's loft 20, 20
Sailmaker's stitches
    roping 21
    seam 21
Sailmaker's tools
    fid 20
    knife 20
    leather seamer palm 20
    needles and needle holders 20
    pricker 20
    seam rubber 20
    stabber 20
Sail rig maneuverability 22
Sail rigs
    fore-and-aft rig
        advantages of 22
        furled 22
        hoisted 22
        reefed 22
        ships rigged with 22
    square rig
        bending the sail 22
        construction of corners 22
        furling 24
        hoisting 24
        loops or "cringles" 22
        reefing 23
        seamanship with 23, 24
        ships rigged with 22
        spirit sails 23
        studding sails 23
Shares 30, 31
Sharp-shooters, marine guard 30
Shaving dish, wooden 33
Sheathing, copper 13
Shell, block 19
Ship owners 25
Shipyards, colonial 8, 10
    workmen in 10, 10
Shiv, block 19
Shore leave 91
Shot 45; see also Projectiles
Shot gauges 45
Shot lockers 8
Shot storage 41
Shrouds 16, 16, 17, 17
Sight vane, quadrant 60
Signals
    Continental Jack 57
    false fires 58
    lanthorn 57
    light flashes 57
    passwords 57
    pendant 57
    shirts off, after boarding 57
    used by privateer pack 57
"Silk socks gentry" 37
Simpkins, Captain William 91
"Skunk", ketch 45
Sloop 21
Small, Captain William
    ship captured 80
Small stuff 15, 52
Smuggling, fast ships for 9
Snuff box, made aboard "Jersey" 87
Songs
    chanteyman 53
    "Manly", a favorite song 53
    pulling songs
        double-pull chanties 53
        single-pull chanties 53
    windlass or capstan chanties 53
    working song 53
Sounds on shipboard
    bo'sun's pipe 34
    "calls" or "pipes" 34
    captain's orders 34
    captain's speaking trumpet 34
"Spanish Town Papers" 23

Spar
    construction
        hewing square 14
        octagonal beveling 14
        rounding 14
    length, rule of thumb concerning 14
    pickling 14
    weight consideration 10
Spare-time craftsmanship of privateer crews
    clam rake 52
    decorative small stuff 52
    fish hooks and hitch 52
    fish or eel spear 52
    horn decoration 52
    pipe, smoking 52
Spear, eel or fish 52
Speed, estimation of enemy's 66
"Speedwell", privateer 88
"Spider catchers"
    armament 8
    crew size 8
    favorite haunts 8
    flotilla 8
    oar and sail 8
    prizes 8
Spindle collar, capstan 37
Spiral auger 12
Splices, eye 17, 36
Sponger, cannon 48
Spritsails 23
Spuryarn, or small cord 17
"Spy", Connecticut schooner 85
Spyglass, Captain Hugh Hill's 27
Square rig, 22
Square sails, construction 22
Square sail seamanship 23
Stabber 20
Standing rigging 16, 17
State commissions 25
Staten Island 8
Stays 16
Stealing from American prisoners 81, 82, 83
Stepping mainmast 14
Stern
    finish 13
    name and port on 13
    narrow 9
Stink pot 71, 71
Stoddard, Captain 88
Storage, in privateer 9
Stowage
    aft bulkheads 42
    ballast 42
    berth or lower deck 42
    fore bulkhead 42
    pumps 42
    shot locker 42
Stratford Point 76
Streaks of plank 12, 12
Studding sails 23
Sun dial, pocket compass and 60
Superstitions
    coaxing up a wind 54
    figureheads 54
    general protection 54
    successful voyage 54
    warning unheeded 54
Surgery
    after engagement 79
    battle preparations for 78
    bedding 78
    capital instruments 78
    during action 79
    equipment 78
    light for 78
    platform 78
    suggestions for 79
Surgical instruments
    amputation saw 78
    crooked needle and waxed thread 78
    retractor 78
    scalpel 78
    screw tourniquet 78
    tenaculum 78
Swab 77
"Swallow", privateer 88
Sweeps 67
Swivel guns 49, 50, 89
    grips 50
    "horn", wrought iron 50
    size 50
    use 50
"Sword", privateer 69

T

Tacking 23
Tampion, cannon 48

Tar, clothing 30
Tarred hemp 15
Telescopes 66
Teredo or seaworm 90, 90
Thole pin, wooden 67
"Three Brothers", British privateer 76
Tibbetts, Captain 88
Topmen
    advice for 39
    battle preparation of 69, 70
Tory refugees 88
Tree-nails (trunnels) 12
"Trooper", privateer brig 57
Trousers, bell-bottom 32
Trumpet, captain's speaking 34
"Tumble home", hull 9

U

Utensils from H.M.S. "Augusta" 52

V

"V" bottom hulls 9
"Vengeance", privateer schooner 57
Vernier, quadrant 60
Victuals
    "Bill of Fair" aboard "Porus" 50
    British Naval Regulations of 1790 50
    dried potatoes 51
    given American captives 82, 83, 85
    hard tack 51
    hard tack recipe 51
    lobscouse, a favorite meal 51
    Massachusetts state navy orders
        of 1776 50
    pewter mug 51
    preserved meat ("salt junk") 50
    rum
        daily ration 51
        "Nelson's blood" 51
Vineyard Sound 8

W

Wallabout Bay, New York 85
Watches
    dog watches 38
    "double shifts" 38
    "idlers" 39
    larboard-starboard 38
    watch billet 38
    watch times 38
Waterproofing
    clothing 30
    hull 12
    rigging 17
Weighing anchor, tools and procedures for
    anchor 37
    anchor cable 36, 36
    bitt 36, 36
    cable 36, 36
    cable crisis 38
    cable hatch 36, 36, 37
    capstan 36, 37
        pawls 37
        spindle collar 37
    cathead 37
    deck stopper 36
    eye splices 36
    "fishing" 37
    hawsepipes 37
    messenger 36, 36, 37, 37
    "nipper boys" 37
    windlass and bars 36
Weight, considerations of on privateers 10
Whaleboats, privateer 8
Whipple, Captain Abraham 91, 91
Whistle, officer's pewter 68
"Whitby", British prison ship 85
Wind 64
"Windage", cannon bore 45
Wind, failing 67
Windlass and bars 36
Windlass chanties 53
Woodbury, Captain 88
Workmen, shipyard 10, 10
Worming iron 49
Worming, standing rigging 17
Wren, Rev. (minister helping
    Forten prisoners) 85

Y

"Yankee", privateer sloop captured 80
Yard rig, lower 18
Yards (spars) 18
Yarns, rope 15
"Young Neptune", privateer schooner 57